Desert, Wilderness, Wasteland and Word

Desert, Wilderness, Wasteland and Word

A New Essay by Jacques Ellul and Five Critical Engagements

Jacques Ellul

Edited by
Michael Morelli

Translated by
Kelsey Hackett

James Clarke & Co.

C

I love to the farthest desert and back.
- Hunter Jack James Morelli

James Clarke & Co.
P.O. Box 60
Cambridge
CB1 2NT
United Kingdom

www.jamesclarke.co
publishing@jamesclarke.co

Paperback ISBN: 978 0 227 18009 9
PDF ISBN: 978 0 227 18010 5

British Library Cataloguing in Publication Data
A record is available from the British Library

First published by Pickwick Publications, 2023

This edition published by James Clarke & Co., 2024,
by arrangement with Wipf and Stock Publishers

Contents

Contributors

Amy J. Erickson (PhD, University of Aberdeen) teaches theology and ethics at St. Mark's National Theological Centre in Canberra, Australia. She is the author of *Ephraim Radner, Hosean Wilderness, and the Church in the Post-Christendom West* (Brill, 2020).

Kelsey Haskett holds a PhD in French literature from Laval University, in Quebec City. She is professor emerita of world languages and cultures at Trinity Western University. In 2011, she published a major study in French on family relationships in Marguerite Duras's novels, entitled *Dans le miroir des mots (In the Mirror of her Words)* (Summa, 2011). She is also the co-editor of a book with Holly Faith Nelson on *French Women Authors: The Significance of the Spiritual (1400–2000)* (University of Delaware Press, 2012). Her main areas of research are French women's literature and works that focus on spiritual perspectives in French literature and thought.

Emily Beth Hill (PhD, University of Aberdeen) is the author of *Marketing and Christian Proclamation in Theological Perspective* (Fortress/Lexington, 2021). Before becoming a theologian she spent ten years in international marketing research. Her research interests include economics, surveillance, social justice, and how cultural systems affect our worship in the church. Emily lives in Cincinnati, Ohio.

Jason Hudson holds a PhD in theology from Cliff College and is an adjunct professor at Cincinnati Christian University. His current work seeks to bring the thought of Jacques Ellul and Wendell Berry into confrontation with current attitudes toward progress, particularly within the context of evangelical Christianity. Beyond mere academic curiosity, his current interests rise out of an effort to bring his theological and philosophical thought into harmony with his roles as a church leader, professor, amateur farmer, and political dissident.

Michael Morelli is assistant professor of theology & ethics at Northwest Seminary & College, a founding member of ACTS Seminaries, an affiliate of Trinity Western University. He holds a PhD in theological ethics from the University of Aberdeen, Scotland, and is the author of *Theology, Ethics, and Technology in the Work of Jacques Ellul and Paul Virilio: A Nascent Theological Tradition* (Lexington, 2021). He publishes and presents on a variety of topics within the fields of theology, morality, culture, politics, and technology. He has also worked in local church ministry and continues to serve the church in a lay capacity.

Jacob Marques Rollison (PhD, University of Aberdeen) is an independent scholar living and working at L'Abri, in Ollond, Switzerland. He is the author of *A New Reading of Jacques Ellul: Presence and Communication in the Postmodern World* (Lexington, 2020). He has recently translated Ellul's two-volume ethical treatise, *To Will & To Do.*

Rev. Dr. G. P. Wagenfuhr is dean of program innovation at the Flourish Institute of Theology and the theology coordinator for ECO: A Covenant Order of Evangelical Presbyterians. He is the author of *Plundering Eden* (Cascade, 2020) and *Plundering Egypt* (Cascade, 2016), both of which were influenced by Jacques Ellul. His PhD from the University of Bristol focused on Jacques Ellul's understanding of the religiosity of social structures and the role of Christians. He lives in Colorado with his wife and two-year-old daughter where he also fabricates custom bicycles.

Introduction

Into the Desert, Wilderness, and Wasteland

A Word of Warning and Encouragement concerning In/Visible Life and Death

Michael Morelli

Finding, editing, translating, and studying Jacques Ellul's desert manuscript was an archaeological discovery, dig, restoration, and viewing. Two editors and one translator lifted this essay's pieces out of the Ellul family archives, brushed off what they found, and fused the fragments. Seven theologians studied what was assembled and wrote down what they saw. What I observed at various stages in the production of this volume has been a timely, communal, and apocalyptic-prophetic answer to the question God asks the priestly-prophet Ezekiel in the Valley of Dry Bones: "Mortal, can these bones live?" (Ezek 37:3). Ellul's essay and each piece engaging with it echoes Ezekiel's response in a unique, provocative way. We collectively say, "O Lord GOD, you know" (Ezek 37:3), but we say it in different ways. The surface appearances of our respective deserts with dry bones differ from Ezekiel's, but the deeper, foundational ideologies and idolatries producing the death-filled deserts are identical. As we learn from Ezekiel, other stories in Scripture, and many stories today, whenever people worship a god who is not the God of Abraham, Isaac, and Jacob, desert valleys materialize and they start getting filled with in/visible death.

Fortunately, Ezekiel's story in chapter 37 *starts* with in/visible death. It *ends* in in/visible life. The positive side of the negative theological-ethical warning about ideology and idolatry offered above is captured in God's response to Ezekiel's reply to God's initiatory question about dry bones: "Prophesy to these bones [Ezekiel], and say to them: O dry bones, hear the Word of the Lord. Thus says the Lord GOD to these bones: I will cause breath to enter you, and cover you with skin, and put breath in you, and you shall live; and you shall know that I am the LORD" (Ezek 37:3–7). Ezekiel's story can become our story, but only if we are willing to do what Ezekiel did when the Lord God communicated with him in the death filled desert valley: speak prophetically to dry bones with hope that the Lord God will appear in the midst of death and be the God who speaks words of life.

Robert Jenson's well-known meditation on the Ezekiel 37 scene consequently emerges as a theological frame for this volume. In the introduction to *Theology in Outline*, Jenson writes the following about this harrowing and hopeful Ezekiel scene:

> The church and its thinking—its theology—begins with that little group of Jews who became convinced that Jesus' resurrection was God's own answer to the question the Lord posed to Ezekiel. They declared the dead bones of God's people, Israel, and the dead bones of humanity in general can indeed live again. Jesus' first disciples thought they should pass on this news. Death does not win, they said.[1]

Ellul and each contributor to this volume echo Jenson's definition of the church's theology as articulated here, but in ways that formulate apocalyptic, prophetic proclamations in the desert, wilderness, and wasteland of today; a desert that, as Ellul so often reminds readers in his work, is a desert of our own making:

> Such valid human activities as political involvement and business become works of death and sin when they are shut into a world which has excluded God in order to glorify, to force, to seduce men. This is no reason to believe that perversion reigns only in the city, that outside her gates business, government, and money are sanctified! But in her we can certainly see the major perversion. Besides, without the city, where would business and government be? In any case, the city has chosen her special role by specifically and voluntarily shutting herself off from any divine intervention.

1. Jenson, *Theology in Outline*, 11–12.

> Stubbornly, obstinately, of her own will, she applies all her attention to herself. And her world without God is also a world of gods. If the desert is the place of demons, the city is the place of idols.[2]

As earthly cities sprawl outwards and upwards, reinforce their walls, stockpile arms, pillage land, pollute water, go to war, and worship the gods Mammon and Mars, the demonic desert grows. The 'chosen' few generate money and power and the harassed and abandoned 'unelect' suffer and cry out. With such stark realities in view, Ellul and each contributor describes why such suffering and death *apparently* Are winning today, yet they follow up such descriptions with prophesies that confidently proclaim suffering and death *assuredly will not* win, despite any appearance to the contrary. In this way, every author offers us the gift of an essay that exposes all mirages of hope in the desert, and inspires an apprehension—a revelation even—of true, communal, bone, flesh, and blood, hope in the God of Abraham, Isaac, and Jacob, the kind of God who shows up, journeys with us, and cares for us in the desert.

With all of the above said, I will share the word of warning and encouragement to which the title of this introductory essay alludes. First, the warning. You may prematurely close this book if you are hoping for a completely coherent theology and ethics that immediately orients you in a disorienting desert valley. But, and now the word of encouragement, persist through the disorientation! Keep reading through the incoherence! As you continue reading, keep a firm grasp on a hope that the incoherent theology and ethics will cohere, precipitate a hearing of God's Word, and provoke a worshipful response from you, the reader who I hope is willing to experience a moment of disorientation in order to hear God's reorienting Word in the desert, wilderness, and wasteland of today.[3]

As Ellul articulates in the essay that lays the foundations for this book, true worship of the God revealed in the Holy Scriptures only appears when people are willing to leave behind all they count as coherent religion. "From the moment [we] stop trying to understand this God and to build a coherent theology, the only possible relationship is worship," Ellul writes.[4] He

2. Ellul, *Meaning of The City*, 54.

3. When I use the terms orientation, disorientation, and reorientation here I have in mind Walter Brueggemann's work on orientation, disorientation, and reorientation in *The Message of the Psalms* and John Swinton's use of these themes in the chapter "Finding God in the Darkness," from *Finding Jesus in the Storm*.

4. Ellul, "Desert," 30.

continues: "Worship [is] the humbling of the mind, knowledge, [and] philosophy" as "entering into worship becomes the opening of the self to the one whom we recognize without knowing."[5] How is it that one would recognize God without knowing God; apprehend God without entering into a relationship with God, let alone worshiping God? One of Jesus' rebukes of the religious leaders of his day offers an answer to this question. The pharisees rebuked in chapter 23 of Matthew's Gospel are depicted as constructing and propagating a coherent theology that manages the people and the world they are in. This construction, propagation, and management helped the pharisees accumulate power, but the cost was a warping of themselves and a damaging of others. To such coherence–and power-addicted managers of people and the world, Jesus presents the following lament: "Woe to you, scribes and Pharisees, hypocrites! *For you are like whitewashed tombs, which on the outside look beautiful, but inside they are full of the bones of the dead and of all kinds of filth.* So you also on the outside look righteous to others, but inside you are full of hypocrisy and lawlessness" (Matt 23:27, emphasis added). Not all dry and filthy bones are discovered in desert valleys. Not all infertile and hostile desert climates are external. Rotten bones and infertile climates like these can be internal, inside people like these pharisees. Inside people like you and I.

Is there any hope for the rebuked pharisees and people like us? To answer this question, let's return to the question God poses to Ezekiel in chapter 37. Can dry, filthy bones be clean again and brought back to life? Can infertile and hostile climates become resting places for God's fertility and peace? Only if there is worship inspired by the kind of incoherent, apocalyptic-prophetic theology and ethics that materializes when the presence, work, and words of the enfleshed Son of God are not only apprehended, but received with reverence and a willingness to go anywhere with this God at anytime, no matter the circumstances—including venturing with this God into the desert, where time dilates and contracts, space expands and constricts, and nothing is certain except the past promises of God that will be realized at some point, either in the present or the future.

Will you enter this kind of desert with us, reader?

We hope you will.

Now, a brief cartography of this book to guide you as we enter the desert, wilderness, and wasteland.

5. Ellul, "Desert," 30.

A Brief Cartography

The first chapter features Ellul's essay titled "The Desert," which appears to have been written in 1977. It was never finished or published until now, in fragmentary form. Jean-Philippe Qadri, the editor of the original French version of this essay, masterfully pieced together the fragments of Ellul's work. Qadri was able to fill in many empty spaces in the primary manuscript with content he discovered in a variety of folders housed in the Ellul family archives. He also provided many helpful annotations to contextualize certain pieces of Ellul's work and guide readers in places where they might otherwise be lost. Likewise, the translator of this essay, Kelsey Haskett, excelled at the difficult work of moving a text out of its original language and into a new language, while keeping the words on the page as reflective of the author's original voice and intent as possible. I am grateful for their work, which I am confident the reader will benefit from greatly.

The form and content of "The Desert" essay will be familiar to anyone acquainted with Ellul's theological-ethical work, but the incomplete form of this piece, combined with the jarring tone and content, will likely create space for a unique encounter with the prolific Ellul writing in his most apocalyptic style. By *apocalyptic*, I mean the kind of apocalyptic-messianism fleshed out by theological ethicist Hans Ulrich in his book *Transfigured Not Conformed*: "To be made a witness is to have any perceptions of the self or of the phenomena that obscure or obliterate God's own actions ripped away,"[6] Ulrich writes. "The paradox of deliverance is that in it phenomena that seemed incontrovertibly real are exposed as fundamentally indeterminate. Seemingly stable and nonnegotiable realities are interrupted and *unveiled* in their ephemerality."[7] For this reason, Ulrich concludes, "[The apocalyptic-messianic aspect of God's word] is an act of witness to having made the transition from thinking and reflecting on human agency and its sources and conditions to the recognition of God's own reality and agency, that is, to God's own ethos within which His partners or children participate. It is in this way that we become witnesses to God's story."[8] As I see it, the gift of Ellul's essay resides in its offering the kind of witness mapped out by Ulrich here. "The Desert" essay is far from clean, predictable, and manageable. It is wild like the desert it pulls readers into. But its

6. Ulrich, *Transfigured Not Conformed*, 36–37.
7. Ulrich, *Transfigured Not Conformed*, 36–37.
8. Ulrich, *Transfigured Not Conformed*, 37.

mess, unpredictability, and unruliness can cause a transition from shallow, navel-gazing treatises on what can be accomplished by human efforts in the wasteland of today to explosive, life-bestowing recognitions of the God who invites us into a story that simultaneously surpasses, enters into, levels, and rebuilds human stories and efforts in a wasteland that could be re-wilded with the generative presence of God.

Amy Erickson's chapter works with the strains in Ellul's essay that force into view the human actions that produce the kinds of deserts described earlier in the passage from *Meaning of The City*. Technology as this age's human action *par excellence* is analyzed by Erickson to expose and undo the ways technologies can produce a human-made wasteland where isolation, loneliness, and impotence abound. Not content to end with a bleak account of the human situation, however, Erickson contrasts this wasteland with a hopeful word about "the biblical wilderness" (38) and the "ecclesial reservoirs" (43) of resurrection, Sabbath, and Eucharist, all meeting together in a "rhythmic resting together and feasting together" as we "prepare to suffer together" (57) in the desert of our day.

Gregory Wagenfuhr's chapter ruminates on Ellul's mid-career contention that God has abandoned the world to itself and chosen silence, offsetting this claim with other facets of Ellul's writing that describe a totally transcendent God who enters into creation and history to liberate both. From these foundations, Wagenfuhr builds upon Ellul's work on liberation in the desert by offering an ecclesial, eschatological, and ecological account of the Promised Land to come, crowning an eco-eccleisial-eschatology with the following proclamation of recapitulation: "[Recapitulation] is the inclusion of all diverse stories of each subatomic particle in the person of Jesus Christ as God becomes king over all creation" (74). He concludes with a word of challenge lest people receive Wagenfuhr's words on recapitulation as permission to wait passively until God's shows up to take us home: "Recapitulation is the mission of the church because it is the reconciling of all things in Christ. Recapitulation is fundamentally ecological in that it is aimed at the liberation of creation from all sin" (74). So, Wagenfuhr pushes for a *participatory* recapitulation in which Christians do not deny the alarming burgeoning barrenness around them but see it and respond with appeals to God for help as they start to act in accordance with God's fruitful presence and action in the deserts of our making.

Emily Hill's chapter fills the sails of Erickson's and Wagenfuhr's chapters as it takes a serious look at the ways churches in North America are starting to watch and manage in the wasteland. The word *watch* is important here, because Hill elaborates her deep concern with the ways surveillance capitalism's techniques and logics have started shaping how church bodies perceive themselves, the world, and so interact internally and externally. With this phenomenon in view, Hill asks the critical theological-ethical question: "Will churches wait patiently for the Word of God to stream into the wild and make a new way to the land of milk and honey, or will they cling to what they know to survive and make ends meet on their own terms?" (78). Fleshing out her answer to this question, Hill exposes surveillance capitalism for what it is—human resource management that plays god in order to get along without God—and responds with a theological-ethical counterclaim that "to hear the Word of God in the desert, to be healed of our alienation, and to discover a new way forward, will require churches to give up the power they have" (91). For, "Only God's Word can bring about transformation in the desert, and though the wait can be agonizing, the promises is certain and the work of God is always a movement from slavery to liberation" (91). In other words, Hill shows via her engagement with Ellul's essay how surveillance capitalism's power enslaves and the God who guides Israel through the desert with pillars of cloud and fire liberates.

Jason Hudson's chapter throws Hill's essay into relief as it, like Erickson's essay, examines how technology can produce the kind of desert that expands without limit and destroys fertile wildernesses and creaturely existence. For Hudson, this phenomenon forms a dialectic "in which the technological orientation of the city is linked with power and control while the orientation of the wilderness is linked with freedom and trust borne of powerlessness" (98). Far from advocating a romanticist retreat to pristine, idealized nature, Hudson argues, "We must dispel the illusion of pristine wilderness" (104) because there is little of the earth left untouched by technique's tendrils. On the other hand, the tendrils can be cut off *anywhere* and liberation borne by trusts and powerlessness can take place *anytime*: "Wilderness can be experienced in urban environments and even in the contemplation of the wildness of humanity" (104). But such wilderness only appears with wilderness disciplines like degrowth, silence, and listening and discerning the Word of God, where we, like Elijah might hear God's whisper.

Jacob Marques Rollison's chapter concludes the volume with an exhortation to flee to the desert, be silent, and pray without ceasing. Like Hudson, Marques Rollison sees the story of Elijah's hearing God's whisper as instructive for those of us who feel as dejected, tired, and lonely as Elijah did in the desert. Resting in this biblical territory, Marques Rollison's theological-ethics for living and dying in the desert rage like the wind that breaks the mountain rocks, shakes like the earthquake and burns like the fire that Elijah encountered, none of which are God's presence, but precede's God's presence eventually manifested in a subtle, quiet voice asking: "What are you doing here[?]" (1 Kings 19:9). As Marques Rollison concludes in his reading and application of this story, "Only by attuning himself to the softly spoken divine command can Elijah be prepared to discern the divine calling for his attention" (124). Only here with this posture, Marques Rollison tells us, might we know that "God's quiet speech is God's loving presence" (125). In this way, Marques Rollison's essay, and this volume, ends not with a bang, but a whisper; a quiet, loving voice calling out in the desert, extending an invitation to a conversation with God, to enlivening prayer with God and with whoever else is there to listen to God with us.

Enlivening Breath

Each essay in this volume sounds out a prophetic word to dry bones in a desert valley. Speaking as the editor of this volume, I hope all the dry bones in the desert of a world emerging from COVID-19, a world navigating significant uncertainty and instability, would receive the enlivening breath of the God who appeared to Ezekiel in the midst of a desert valley filled with death, and extended an offer of life.

Bibliography

Brueggemann, Walter. *The Message of the Psalms: A Theological Commentary*. Minneapolis: Augsburg Fortress, 1984.

Ellul, Jacques. *The Meaning of The City*. Translated by Dennis Pardee. Eugene, OR: Wipf & Stock, 2011.

Jenson, Robert. *Theology in Outline: Can These Bones Live?* New York: Oxford University Press, 2016.

Swinton, John. "Finding God in the Darkness." In *Finding Jesus in the Storm: The Spiritual Lives of Christians with Mental Health Challenges*, 89–116. Grand Rapids: Eerdmans, 2020.

Ulrich, Hans. *Transfigured Not Conformed: Christian Ethics in a Hermeneutical Key*. London: T. & T. Clark, 2022.

Chapter One

The Desert[1]

Jacques Ellul

'A Preliminary Remark on' Biblical Vocabulary[2]

Among the Hebrew words for "desert,"[3] I will mention two: one, which is by far the least common, is *yeshimon* (ישימון), which means *solitude*

1. I use initials in footnotes to designate who has written the content because two editors and one translator worked on this manuscript. Jean-Philippe Qadri is listed as J-P.Q.; Kelsey Haskett as K.H.; and myself as M.M.

J-P.Q. "The Desert," an unpublished manuscript from family archives, ff. 1–10 + 4 ff. not numbered, placed in an envelope with a postmark indicating the year 1977. The notion of the "human desert" also appears in Ellul, *New Demons*, 131.

K.H. This text on the desert has now been published as ch. 15 of Ellul's *Vivre et penser la liberté* [*Living and Thinking Freedom*].

M.M. As noted by J-P.Q. and K.H., the unpublished manuscript is titled "The Desert," so it is important to specify that this volume, not Ellul's original essay, is titled *Desert, Wilderness, Wasteland, and Word.* I felt the latter title poetically communicates central themes of Ellul's essay, while also capturing the foci of the critical engagements comprising this volume.

2. K.H. A number of passages in this text were written by Ellul as notes, rather than full sentences. The editor of the original French version, Jean-Philippe Qadri, has expanded these to sentence form, using single stroke quotation marks to indicate the words he has added for the sake of clarity or fluidity. He has done the same with headings and subheadings he has added in part or in whole.

3. K.H. The French word *désert* can be translated both as *desert* and *wilderness* in English. The two words are used in this translation, both to reflect their usage in certain well-known biblical passages and to bring out nuances that may differentiate the desert, with its specific geographical features, from the wilderness, with often broader implications. However, both words may be used metaphorically, and are often used interchangeably, both here and in biblical passages.

or *waste land*—basically 'caused by' human action. The other is *midbar* (מדבר), whose root is *dabar, the word* (essentially the word of God), *speech*, or *promise*. From there all the combinations exist within two streams of thought:

- The word which resonates in the desert. Because it is received in the desert, it implies this desert. The word can only be heard well in the desert (one is faithful). The promise only has its fullest meaning in the desert (elsewhere it is smothered by all that fills our lives).
- The word that cries in the wilderness (for the one who hears it, or for the surroundings).

Whatever it may be, the tie between word and desert is fundamental. Obviously in understanding what the *origin* of this connection could have been, one can take *two directions*: either *the tie between the two words was first of all a given*, and all the biblical narratives in which we see the people or prophet going to the desert to receive the word are built on this. Or else, *the language follows the historical experience*: the people (and Abraham) learn through experience that in every case it is in the desert that they receive the Revelation, and therefore establish the linguistic relationship between the two terms. 'This study will consist of two parts': that which is stated in the biblical text, and then the theological perspective (with the spiritual desert, the theological desert, and the Ethics of the desert).[4]

I—What the Bible States

I. 'The Place of Temptation and Meeting'

A first glance at the texts (outside of the narratives to be studied) shows us the desert *as an essentially ambiguous place*. The desert is *both good and bad*: *good* because it is the place to which God sends man or man encounters God; but at the same time *bad* because it is a place of absence, deprivation, void, and chaos. Thus, it signifies *both* a promise and a threat: "I will bring you back to the desert"[5] (towards Israel's first experience of encountering

4. M.M. Ellul often uses capitals and lowercases, punctuation, and typographic emphases inconsistently in unpublished manuscripts. Although it is tempting to 'correct' these inconsistences, we have chosen to represent Ellul's work as close to 'as written' as possible.

5. J-P.Q. Cf. Hos 2:16; 12:10.

God), but also, in numerous texts, "I will reduce the land to a desert" (Ps. 107:33; Hosea 2:3). And the final promise is precisely that there will be no more desert, that the desert itself will become fertile (Isa. 32:15; 35:1, 6; 43:19–20; 51:3; Joel 2:22; Ps. 107:35). The desert is at the same time the place of the devil and demons, *and* of encountering God (Hosea 3:5). This association probably comes from the idea that is common to all Semitic peoples that the desert is a place of spirits (*djinn*).[6] But here the 'meaning' is much more extreme because it is all or nothing (*cf.* the scapegoat and the column of fire). A final aspect of duality remains: the desert is *the place of man's weakness*, of the absence of food, of solitude; and at the same time it is *the place of man's initiative*, of conquest, and the point of departure for the human adventure—totally touching the sociological 'domain'—but all founded on the searching of the soul.

II. 'Biblical Texts on the Desert'

Next, the biblical narratives in which the desert is an essential place can be taken on a simply descriptive level [knowing that I am not seeking, from a biblical point of view, to provide a theological update to the Jewish thinking on the desert between the eighth and second centuries before Christ. I take the texts exactly as they are, in their theological rather than historical sequence. But I do not do a dogmatic analysis that is simply confirmed by the texts: I prefer to take the texts themselves in large units and to let them speak, as they weave a whole for us, with the constant interplay of references coming from each of the narratives and causing a progressive pattern to appear.][7]

1. Creation—The first mention of the desert is found in the story of the

K.H. In many references to biblical texts, the author is summing up an idea, even if he uses quotation marks. The verses referenced from the French Bible (probably a version of the Louis Second Bible) are occasionally numbered differently from the verses found in English translations (for example, throughout Hosea). I have translated Ellul directly, and not changed the verse numbers he cites, except in cases where a particular English version is quoted (NCV, NIV, or NLT), because its meaning closely reflects the French.

6. J-P.Q. One of the words the Koran uses to designate *demons* and other *spirits*. According to Paul Ballanfat, "Genies," 981, "genie" [spirits] were considered demigods in pre-Islamic Arabia. They were nymphs and satyrs living in the desert and they represented the threatening side of nature.

7. J-P.Q. Note from an independent folio.

creation (Gen. 1:2) where not only chaos (*tohubohu*) but also the desert is brought into play: the earth is "formless and void"—and the Spirit of God is moving on the surface of the waters. We need to trace the logical contradiction: the earth is already there, and yet God creates it (v. 9–10); there are already waters, although God creates (v. 9–10). But this reveals two things: first, the desert is a place of contradiction—and also of all possibilities. Everything is blended together. Everything is virtual: the formlessness and the void is that which can give birth to form and which is waiting to be filled. The desert is the place of waiting for the accomplishment, so it is natural that it has a connection to the promise.

The promise is spoken in and over the desert. And it is the first tie between the word and the desert: the word of God is that which alone can give shape to and fill this absolute void.

The other aspect of this text resides in the "creation." It is common 'to interpret this passage' according to Greek philosophy and creation *ex nihilo*. 'However, creation is' never 'mentioned' in the Bible. All that is shown is the act of separation (and *barah* really means *fabrication*). There is "something" when God creates: no enlightenment on a point zero, but only that which is necessary for us to recognize who is our God. He brings order to the chaos; he fills the desert with his word—that is, he gives meaning to absence. But it is not only a negative absence: it is an absence that is there, an insignificance that is substantial (just as Death is an active power). Thus, what is negative is still something: the desert.[8]

2. Abraham—The second mention of the desert concerns Abraham, at the time of his departure from Ur (Gen. 12:1–4). This already establishes the importance of the desert, which is situated first at the starting point of creation and then at the starting point of the election.

Abraham is called to leave the fertile crescent and cross the desert to enter into the land which God gives. This journey is sometimes interpreted as an initiation rite; in reality, it marks the stretch of desert between what one leaves and what God gives—between the world, society, humanity, civilization, and the kingdom of God. The kingdom of God is not in the same place as we are. The kingdom of God is not in continuity with what we are doing: a rupture is needed, an abandon. The transition to the desert

8. M.M. For further commentary on Ellul's interpretation of the creation accounts in Genesis 1 and 2, particularly as they concern the doctrine of *creation ex nihilo* as mentioned here, see Ellul, *On Freedom, Love, and Power*, 22–23. Ellul also discusses this in the untranslated *La Genèse aujourd'hui* (*Genesis Today*).

is a transition to absence, to nothingness, on the simple declaration of the Word of God, to receive something unknown: in fact, it is not specifically said in the call that the promised land will be better or superior (this will be added much later): what he will find beyond the desert is not necessarily more that what he has lost. God promises him a country "that I will show you,"[9] so it is not even known in advance. And in reality, all that is confirmed four times in two verses is the Blessing: the good word that God speaks. Abraham has nothing else with which to cross the desert but the Word of God. Thus, the desert is identified with a questioning of faith, radical or not, in this Word.

3. Ishmael—The third mention of the desert concerns Ishmael (Gen. 16:17 and 21), the counterpart of both Abraham and Isaac (*yišmāʿ ēʾl* means *God will hear*).

Birth in the desert is the counterpart inherent in the disobedience of Abraham ('bringing about the promise' by himself)—and the opposite to his former obedience: the desert here reveals the temptation to substitute oneself for God. Ishmael chooses to be a wild man amongst men (*pere adam*),[10] a wild man born in the desert and who wants to live in the desert which he chooses (Gen. 21:20). By doing this he is exempt from any "place"—proof that nomadism in itself is not holy! But Ishmael and the desert also signify the absence of a future. Isaac, whose name means *he will laugh*, is situated in time. There is a future for him, a plan orientated by the promise. While Ishmael 'is also characterized by laughter, this laughter is defined' by the present: "he laughs" (Gen. 21:9). Ishmael sneers, with the laughter of bitterness and mocking. The desert here is the absolute dominance of the immediate, the present without any depth. A situation outside of Time and Place.

But God meets Ishmael, as well, in the desert. For not only did God "hear" 'the distress of Hagar his mother' (Gen. 16:11), as well as the 'prayer of Abraham for Ishmael,' ("I heard you," Gen. 17:20), but "God heard the

9. J-P.Q. Compare Gen 12:2–3 (Abraham's departure from "his country" for "the country" that God will show him, without other details) with Gen 13:15 (first mention of the large expanse of land, but still limited to what a person can see) and Gen 15:18 (the expanse of land henceforth going beyond human limits because it goes "from the River of Egypt to the Great River").

10. J-P.Q. In his commentary on the Torah, Rashi of Troyes interprets the prophecy over Ishmael in Gen 16:12 ("He will be a wild man" (*hāyâ pere' 'āḏām*) by the fact that "he will be a man of the desert."

cries of the boy" (Gen. 21:17). However, even if God receives this weeping, even if Ishmael is not abandoned (as compared to Cain), even if he is helped, and even if this desert he chooses is not an obstacle between him and God, he is not led there by God to receive the word of God (new ambiguity).

4. Moses—Now comes the explicit meeting with God in the desert (Exod. 3; 5:1–3), which allows God to be named the "God of the desert." First of all, it is in the desert that God reveals himself and gives his name[11] (thereby showing a progression: after his secretive action comes the revelation). Moses chances to go the desert, to feed his flocks; there is no deliberate choice or memorial act. Now on this occasion, when he is separated from everything by the desert, he receives a double revelation:

- On the one hand, the knowledge of the Holy Land: God isn't from a place built by man, in the midst of men; the desert alone is likely to be the place 'claimed by God' because there can be no confusion there, no misunderstanding: the "nothingness" becomes holy because God is there and the desert marks a "separation" from everything else (holiness);[12]

11. J-P.Q. Exod. 6:3 (NLT): "I appeared to Abraham, to Isaac, and to Jacob as El-Shaddai—'God Almighty'—but I did not reveal my name, Yahweh, to them."

12. M.M. Ellul often points out *holiness* means *otherness* and *separation* when used to describe God's holiness. For Ellul, this has theological and moral implications for the people of God in that their holiness ought to be a God-derived otherness, or separateness that does not retreat from the world, but lives in and cares for the world in a distinct, God-reflecting way. Capturing the radicality of this holiness in an apocalyptic key, Ellul writes in *To Will and To Do*, 109: "In the wall of morality which man wants to build for himself, behind which he hopes to find shelter from God, there must be a breach for God's will to pass through. It is the tension lived by the Christian between the two moralities in this society which is, of itself, the breach of God, the breach through which God passes, whenever his word causes his requirement to reecho in a life within which the Christian has born witness, in a society in which the Christian has lived, in which he has participated. And when the word is presented so alive that God's requirement is beyond dispute, then the tension can disappear, for the word carries its decisive contradiction to the moral order which can only explode. The choice becomes radical and necessary. There is no longer any obedience which holds to the order of the world. There is a judgment of that order by holiness. The explosion of the revelation destroys the ethic of the world. Whether it is a question of the morality of the individual, his decisions and his choices, or whether it is a question of the moral order of society with its imperatives, ideals, and structures, the tension would be still another compromise and a betrayal if it were the lasting solution to the contradiction. But not this tension itself is continually called into question by the requirement of absolute obedience to, undivided loyalty,

- On the other hand, it will only be in the desert that one will be able to offer sacrifices to God: going to the wilderness becomes an order from that point on (3:18). No worship of God is possible in the cities of Egypt and in the Egyptian temples: this God described by his historical reference (3:6) cannot be compared to any other god (of nature): this is a break with every form of the worship of nature (and society and culture). And it is in relation to this separation, this recusal, that everything will be played out with Pharaoh.

5. Israel in the Desert—Then comes the Exodus, obviously, and the entrance into the desert.

a. We must remember that *Mizraim* (Egypt) is "the land of double anguish" (the anguish of living and dying—or even the anguish of killing and being killed)—which, by those very words, describes the totality of the human condition: slavery, alienation, work alienated . . . in anxiety. The departure from Egypt is the departure from all of that, while the entrance into the desert is very clearly the entrance into both liberty and insecurity. There is, at the same time, an abandonment of the goods, riches, and hardships of Egypt (which are sometimes missed: "let us go back to Egypt")[13] and an entering into liberty.

But before this, the desert is the distance from retrieval, which prevents Pharaoh from taking Israel back (Exod. 13:18). The desert is the place where *the world's power shows itself to be powerless.*

At this point freedom is unfurled: all roads are possible in the desert—this place where the focal point of undefined possibilities is located, this place of endless wandering. Man is not constrained by anything. *But* man cannot live there (any more than he can live in absolute liberty).

b. What makes living in the desert possible is the active presence of God. In his proximity, God on the one hand gives food (this will be a frequent sign;

which the word of God causes to reecho in our lives." Elsewhere, in a more constructive register, he writes in *The Ethics of Freedom*, 7: "Holiness as separation, service, and witness for God, or a conflict of faith, expresses the distinctiveness of incarnate Christianity, but separation has a place only for the sake of mission. The break has to come first, but it implies a rediscovery of the world, society, and one's neighbor in a new type of relationship." Karl Barth's influence is evident in both quotes.

13. J-P.Q. Cf. Num 14:3–4: Man first misses death with the assurances of Egypt: cf. the Egyptian sepulchres and the horror of dying in the desert (Exod 14:11)—then he reveals that he misses its comfort and food (Exod 16:3; 17:3).

cf. Elijah or Jesus divinely fed in the desert)[14] and on the other he shows the way. But in all that there is never anything constrained or obligatory; the only thing in which man is called to trust is the presence of God, as the pillar of fire and the pillar of cloud indicate. The desert is livable precisely to the degree that it is chosen by God for the place of meeting. Because it is a place of perdition (Deut. 8:15; Num. 32:15), the desert is clearly the place where man has no possibility of living by himself: no protection, no institution, no relationship. 'Because the wilderness is the absence of all' human power, man cannot have any illusions about himself, his survival or his success. With God alone, man lacks nothing (Deut. 2:7). But it is still man, by himself, who is called to cross the desert. His work is indispensable (Deut. 2:7).

This presence of God contradicts human expectations (with Pharaoh thinking, in Exod. 14:3, "The Israelites are lost, trapped by the desert" [NCV]) and brings about the essential interruption: in human planning the desert closes in, whereas in God, it is liberty. This is how it is with Christian liberty, because the Commandment is judged and considered by man as a form of slavery! Moreover, the presence of God appears like a contradiction in relation to the environment in which man finds himself: the pillar of fire shines at night, and the pillar of cloud creates the obscurity of the day.

c. The experience of the desert takes place "*so that* you might know that I am the Lord your God" (Deut. 29:6) (NIV). Such an experience is both liberation, risk, initiative, obedience, and the inability to foresee, which engenders faith. And it is this experience that the people of Israel will ceaselessly commemorate, analyse, and study in depth, and on which they will build all their theology. It is in this way that God is a God of the desert! That is, in as much as the period of the desert appears in the prophets as the period when Israel is blessed—not because of the nomadic lifestyle!

But the inverse is also true: God reveals to his people that it is in the wilderness that he found them and chose them (cf. the Song of Moses; Deut. 32:10): it is in the desert-chaos-nothingness of the peoples [of the world] that God discerned this people and led them into a different desert.

14. J-P.Q. On the folio of biblical references connected to this study, Ellul comments: "With a slight variation in pronunciation, 'the same root' can mean desert or pasture." Cf. Isa. 5:17 (דֹּבֶר) and Mic. 2:12 (דֹּבֶר), where the Hebrew word for "pastures" shares the same root דֹּבֶר as "desert-*midbar*" (מִדְבָּר).

With this first series of texts, therefore, we have the essential progression of meanings that the desert contains: from the Creation to the Election, from the Election to Revelation, and from Revelation to Liberation.

d. After the liberation, the constitution of the people as the people of God is described in the fourth book of the Bible, which we call "Numbers," but which is called, in fact, *In the desert-bamidbar* (בַּמִּדְבָּר)—with the play on words, in the first verse, between *davar* and *midbar*, that is, between "word" and "desert."[15] Now, we find there three main themes:

I. Holiness (which is a setting apart of the people), with the treatment of impurity,[16] of purification,[17] of the Nazirite,[18] of the altar, and of sacrifices.[19]

II. Life in the desert, where constant rebellion against God's demands is manifested (looking back to Egypt, the revolts of Miriam[20] and Korah,[21] etc.), as well as ambiguity (the people are saved from serpents by the bronze serpent,[22] from Balak by Baalam's donkey[23])

III. The outcome, as described in chapters 27 (in which the character of Joshua foreshadows that of Jesus) and 28 (in which the sacrifice for life is described,[24] being the offering for life and the announcement of the promised land).

In this book, the desert is the Non-Appropriation, the Non-Establishment. It is the sign of the holiness invested in the Levites, who represent

15. K.H. With a discussion on the prepositional *lamed* (לְ): does "the prepositional *lamed* which figures at the beginning of the word עֲזָאזֵל when it occurs in Leviticus mean 'for'"?

J-P.Q. Cf. Num 1:1 (NIV): "The Lord spoke [דָּבַר] to Moses in the tent of meeting in the Desert [מִדְבָּר] of Sinai on the first day of the second month of the second year after the Israelites came out of Egypt [מִצְרַיִם]."

16. J-P.Q. Num 19.

17. J-P.Q. Num 8:6–21; 19.

18. J-P.Q. Num 6:1–21.

19. J-P.Q. Num 7:15.

20. J-P.Q. Num 12:15.

21. J-P.Q. Num 16.

22. J-P.Q. Num 21:4–9.

23. J-P.Q. Num 22:22–35.

24. J-P.Q. This is the "continual burnt offering" mentioned in Num 28:3, 6, 10, 15, 23–24, 31.

the institution of those who are still in the desert, without city or land, but who live at the expense of others. We understand, therefore, that through them, "the others" participate in the desert, that is to say that one can be an inhabitant, a manager, but not an owner—the affirmation is all the stronger in that the book of Numbers was written *after* the settling of the people of Israel in the promised land: its author is therefore trying to teach a "lesson," the theology of the desert.

6. The Goat of the Desert and the Expiations (the Purification)—Lev. 16:3–34. According to two simple, sociological points of view, these texts bear witness to the ambivalence of the sacred and to a ritual of purification by blood (stemming from magic). In reality, the bull offered as a sacrifice is the image of a false god; it is sacrificed to attest to the holiness of the revealed God. For it clearly has to do with a sacrifice destined to express holiness and to make the people holy (consecrated to the only God).

As for the goat Azazel (עֲזָאזֵל), 'he is "sent into the desert" and "carries all the faults of the people of Israel into an arid place" (16:22). His name raises a question.' We find in the word '*azazel*- עֲזָאזֵל the roots '*ez*—עֵז(goat) and *azal*–אָצַל (to go away), meaning "the goat that goes away." But the first root can also be read as '*oz*–עֹז, that is, "strength, power, fortress, pride."

It is recognized that Azazel is a) the actual name of the goat; b) the place in the desert to which the goat is sent.[25] 'What is important is the connection between this goat that is sent into the desert and' the power: 'not only' is all the disobedience placed on Azazel 'but' the goat is vowed to power. Now, the sacrifice of Lev. 16 is an exact copy of the sacrifice made on the edge of the desert by Balak, king of Moab (Num. 23). 'Effectively,' the sacrifice of Balak is a sacrifice of power and not of expiation and holiness. Moreover, it doesn't take place precisely in the desert,[26] and 'does not produce any' expiation of sin. 'With the bull offered as a sacrifice and' the goat being chosen for God by the casting of lots, the sacrifice of Balak is turned

25. * K.H. With a discussion on the prepositional *lamed* (ל): does "the prepositional *lamed* which figures at the beginning of the word עֲזָאזֵל when it occurs in Leviticus mean 'for'"?

J-P.Q. This is Rachi's reading of Lev 16:8: "'Azazel. It is a mountain that is steep *('az)* and precipitous, a high rock, as it is written: "a country torn apart" (verse 22), that is to say, sharp-edged (Yoma 67b)."

26. J-P.Q. Cf. Num 23:28 (NIV): "And Balak took Balaam to the top of Peor, overlooking the wasteland."

against him. 'By sending away the goat Azazel,' the power is expulsed toward the desert; by him the sin of power is expulsed.[27]

7. The Desert of Elijah—1 Kings 19. The characteristics we have already see are found again in this passage: the choice of the wilderness prevails both as a way to create a distance from the enemy and as a place to encounter God. For Elijah it is about fleeing from the king's men on the one hand (not dying at the hand of Ahab) and putting his life into the hands of God on the other (asking God to take his life). It is both a refuge and an abandonment. Moreover, the wilderness remains the place of impotence, and of recognizing the failure of all human means. The man of action and politics comes to the desert to acknowledge failure. Finally, it is the place of coming face to face with God. Elijah has acted and now, in the wilderness, it is a time of renouncing; the man arrives at the point of recognizing his failure even though he has acted as a prophet (which shows to what degree the prophet is acting on his own decision and initiative: he does not meet God 'permanently;' he doesn't have continuous inspiration). The wilderness thus becomes a time of testing: Elijah comes and presents himself to God and stays 40 days (the time of the temptation), without any response. And finally, he receives the revelation of God who does not act in violence (it is the judgement of what Elijah did with the prophets of Baal), but who acts in secret and charges him with a mode of action that is totally different.

As a result: the wilderness is the place from which one departs for a new mission in society, from where one receives an additional exigency from God. The wilderness becomes a place where history is brought together and prepares to be enacted.

8. The Desert and the Temptation of Jesus[28]—This desert sums up and confirms absolutely all the elements encountered here. After his baptism, Jesus is led by the Spirit into the wilderness.[29]

27. J-P.Q. Sentence crossed out on the manuscript: "The desert is the furnace of the evil power that will destroy."

28. J-P.Q. Cf. Ellul, *If You Are the Son of God*, "The Three Temptations in the Desert," 55–93.

M.M. See also Ellul, *Ethics of Freedom*, 51–66. In both cases, Fyodor Dostoevsky's book *The Brothers Karamazov*, and the story told within that story *The Grand Inquisitor*, influenced Ellul's reading of the desert temptations as outlined here and below.

29. J-P.Q. Cf. Matt 4:1; Mark 1:12; Luke 4:1.

a. The Election takes place (already in the desert, for the Jordan valley is a desert), and the proclamation is immediately followed by a calling into question. And because it is the Spirit that is at the source of it, that means that the desert is the abandonment not only of human means, and human strength, but also of spiritual certainties. This was already the case with Elijah, driven to despair ("I acted according to your word and your will, and it led to nothing"), a despair encompassing the will to die. At the very moment Jesus has just been designated as the Son, he is abandoned by the Father to be subject to Temptation. Alone facing the Tempter, he has no other strength but human strength.

So, the wilderness is the terrible place of total abandonment—with no guarantee that God is there. God comes solely by grace. And in the present case, Jesus will not have the support of the Father (nor a divine nature to protect him).

b. The three temptations of Jesus[30] encapsulate the possible temptations facing man:

- The economic temptation: Jesus, who is hungry, receives the suggestion to miraculously turn stones into bread. This is the modern-day temptation: material temptation, with all the consumerism accompanying it, is the key and justification of all our economic and technical enterprises.
- Political temptation: 'The word of Satan over the kingdoms of the earth ("All this I will give you") shows that the kingship is Satan's. And yet, Jesus came to be recognized as Lord: thus, Satan proposes to do for him exactly what he has been sent for . . .
- The spiritual temptation: ("Show yourself to be the Son of God"). Jesus came precisely to show that God had sent his Son!

30. J-P.Q. Cf. Matt. 4:1–11; Luke 4:1–13.

c. The wilderness is therefore the place where temptation is revealed to be exactly what it is: that is, the incitement for man to take for himself what God wants to give him and to use his own means and strength (Ishmael) to do what God has, in fact, given him to do. In other words, once again, the desert brings to light spiritual reality without ambiguity and without confusion.

In the workplace, the city, the world, all kinds of misunderstanding are possible. Types of confusion between the Word of God and Satan's word 'are numerous': Satan leads us to take the hubbub and activity in the world for the work and Word of God.

d. Four additional comments remain:

- The wilderness is the place where we see the world (the kingdoms) and the needs (hunger) without ambiguity in their identity. It is also, therefore, the point of view *on* . . .
- The wilderness is the place of obedience: Jesus renounces everything to be obedient to the Father (like Elijah). There, he knows nothing but the *objective* Word of God; he abandons both human argument, spiritual power, and his personal relationship with God. Jesus limits himself to obeying his Father absolutely, instead of claiming his status as the Son of God (now, all that is already contained in the Way of the Desert in the Old Testament.)
- The Temptation in the desert precisely prefigures the Cross. 'In the two situations there is the abandonment of Jesus by the Father, and the temptation to be recognized on account of his power ("He trusted in God, let God deliver him now if he loves him, and we will believe in him"), with perfect parallelism—the suffering corresponding to the solitude, like the thirst ("I thirst") to the hunger, or the provocations of men ("Come down from the cross") to those of Satan ("If you are the Son of God").'[31]
- Finally, the wilderness is therefore the place where one lives with human failure at the same time as abandonment by God—the continuous possibility of this abandonment (that of Grace). That which introduces one to the spiritual desert.[32]

31. J-P.Q. Paragraph composed using reorganized notes from f 7.

32. J-P.Q. The last sentence from this part has been crossed out: "In short, the desert is a parable about God himself, his being, and his grace." (f° 7). It refers back to an

II—The Theological Perspective

I. 'From Retreat to Flight'

From there, the way of the desert will haunt the first generations of Christians: Paul, after his conversion, spends several years in the desert to meditate before undertaking his apostleship.[33] Saint Augustine, as well, 'experiences a period of preparation in the desert, as did, more generally,' all the cenobites and Fathers of the desert.[34]

But, as often happens, when starting with a right point of view, there was a distortion and false interpretations.

The wilderness became a voluntary and permanent escape from the world. The withdrawal took place because of a contempt and hatred for the world of corruption. One went to the desert 'not only' to find purity, flee temptations, concentrate (flee distractions), but 'also' to stay. There is no desire to go back to the world afterwards. It is more the attitude of Noah 'than of Paul.'

Reciprocally, the desert became the place for an "abstract" contemplation of God: 'One sought God in and of himself, the essence of God, God as a fixed object of contemplation.

The wilderness also became a place of suffering that men inflicted upon themselves, a place of ascetism and scourging[35]—with a theology of merit necessarily attached to it: one had to conquer the body, the flesh, by the hardest and most deprived life. Added to that was the conviction that evil is outside of me (it is in "the world"; therefore I must separate myself from the world and live in the desert) and outside of the true me (the flesh, which needs to be overcome through asceticism). Inevitably, the desert becomes a means to salvation.

And finally, the wilderness appears as a place outside of History, a place that does not involve history. One lets the world go by as it will. Solitude is useful in itself and the break with humanity 'is salutary.'

---

independent note: "Final. / Globally the desert is a parable for God himself: "My weakness + [only?] man's strength"/ all the possibilities / grace alone. / From which an *analogy* is possible but none / neither Nature / neither Culture / nor "There is . . . " (f° 6v).

33. J-P.Q. Gal 2:17–18.

34. J-P.Q. The cenobites lived apart from the world in community (contrary to hermits and anchorites).

35. J-P.Q. *Le Trésor de la Langue Française* indicates: "Practice of asceticism, privations, and mortifications that one inflicts on one's body, through a spirit of penitence, to submit the flesh to the spirit."

All of this, which leads to a conception of the wilderness as a place outside of History, is derived in part from Greek thought[36] and partly from Hindu thinking (whose influence is certain starting with the second century). One finds a similar concept of the wilderness in Islam. But precisely, none of this has anything to do with the biblical conception.

II. The Human Desert

'Section not included in the final text'[37]

III. The Spiritual Desert

It is the experience of all spiritual life to find itself in the wilderness, that is to say, to live though the silence of God, the night, or abandonment. After having spoken, God is quiet. God turns away from us. Now such an experience, specific to the Christian life, is not comparable to the normal situation of people who do not know God.

36. J-P.Q. Ellul adds in brackets, "(and the typical Greek desert)."

37. J-P.Q. A separate folio contains the following preparatory notes: "The human desert 'is the place' of suffering / of Sickness—of Old Age and Death / of the absence of friends—of the absence of means to live / of the excess of work—of the absence of meaning in life / of the distance between proposed consummation and possible claim of ownership— of the accumulation of meetings /—/ All human deserts are covered by what the Bible says of the desert. / Every human desert has its place within these 5 models (Genesis 'or the desert' without form and void 'as a place of' creation ; Abraham: leaving for the desert, 'place of' election; Ismael: choice of the desert 'or the metaphor of a' cultural God; Moses: the chance of the desert 'or the grace of the' revelation; Israel: the sending into the desert 'or the sign of the' liberation—and Jesus 'in the desert, who sums up all the models') / And in every case, 'there is' temptation //—Out of the human desert, God creates meaning /—God gives a vocation of going through the human wilderness /—God places us in the wilderness in the form of a question addressed to our lives /—God 'opens' a way in the human wilderness as an experience of freedom, life, and of the possible // God lets the wilderness be temptation, along with freedom of faith and responsibility."

a. When one has received the Light of God, or heard his Word, this has relativized and devalued everything else. That is to say that the word of God, living, personal, heard and received as a real revelation from God, reduces everything else to nothing: human values, means, successes, certainties, meanings, relationships, works, thoughts . . . All of that is not only relativized but also, in light of the Word of God, indeed, the presence of God, completely obliterated. In other words, the Word of God places us in the desert.[38] It reduces to nothing all our human pretentions (as Pascal well saw). And nothing has any value except by him ("it is by your light that we see the light"[39]).

b. When this light and this presence are erased, we are in a state of need: it is an absolute desert. For nothing else that is human comes to take its place. God disappears, but 'even with that happening,' that does not return the value of the things of this world. They remain without interest. We are in absolute silence. Now the experience of silence, of absence, of Night is real.

'It is translated by' the fact that prayer not only remains unanswered, but even seems not to be heard. 'It is the feeling of a' prayer that falls into an empty heaven or hits a kind of wall; no more dialogue is possible; one is knocking on a closed door. Such a prayer can continue a whole lifetime in that state: Abraham lived a hundred years 'before becoming a father' and Hannah 'lived through years of suffering without a child, in spite of her prayers' (1 Samuel 1). But the order remains: 'We are asked to' "knock"[40] no matter what—and to pray. Now if prayer were a simple and open dialogue, there would be no need to give the order to "watch and pray."[41] It is because the prayer 'is said' in the silence of God that the order has its reason for existing.

38. J-P.Q. Ellul picks up this idea in his commentary on chapter 12 of Revelation in *Apocalypse*, 90: "But this time in the wilderness is also that which, from this moment onward [that of the Incarnation] begins for humanity (and that is why, from Jesus Christ onward, a ferment of disintegration is introduced into all cultures and civilizations; civilization changes its nature, historically, wherever the Gospel is preached: man enters into the wilderness), it is the new relationship with God that is inaugurated, including that which is unpredictable, uncertain, and not determined—of freedom, in a word."

39. J-P.Q. Ps 36:10.

40. J-P.Q. Matt 7:7; Luke 11:9.

41. J-P.Q. Matt 26:41; Mark 13:33; 14:38.

This is really the wilderness—a wilderness that we have not chosen, or wanted, and where we suffer all the more because this certainty about God becomes incomprehensible. We are, thus, the most unhappy of individuals.

c. But is the abandonment of God possible? Is it not an illusion? Objectively, God does not abandon, because Jesus Christ is always Savior and Lord. As for the felt presence, is it really that important? If Thomism and Calvinism are completely against 'the search for such a felt presence,' does not its absence mean the return to an unobtrusive God, an unchangeable object whose existence is all we try to discover and to proclaim with no more than our personal conviction (cf. Bultmann)? Now, the biblical God is a God who on the one hand enters into History, and therefore accompanies the unfolding of our history, and on the other hand is "God with us."[42] Therefore it is not only on the basis of an objective declaration 'that our spiritual life is founded,' but also on the basis of a living reality in all its dimensions.

d. So 'the question remains': Can God turn away from us and keep quiet? 'To this question we have to reply,' "Yes," since there is a "history," that is a relationship which is not always the same; and because God can turn away from us and remain silent. 'Numerous' biblical texts 'witness to this.' This is what Israel feared the most: we can accept the condemnation of God, and the wrath of God, but the hardest thing to accept is the silence of God and his abandonment. And this silence exists (I Samuel 3:1 "the word of God was rare in those days") and can exist for centuries. Silence can be collective or individual.[43]

The Word of God is not a word said once and for all, which remains objective, like something we have acquired. It must be reactivated in us. But when it does not become alive again, it is dead (and therefore a generator of the negative desert.) Once the Word has become the written word, it is not the Word "of God" except by God, that is, by the Spirit. One cannot make the word become alive by different tricks (such as group dynamics or linguistics): it is only alive by the Holy Spirit. But we are not owners of the Holy Spirit, which can be silent or not be present (without 'this freedom of

42. J-P.Q. Matt 1:23

43. M.M. Ellul's book *Hope in Time of Abandonment* develops this theological theme and marks a significant shift in the architectonic of his thought. As contributor Gregory Wagenfhur notes in his essay, "The Desert: Recapitulating and Going Beyond Ellul," for this volume, Rollison, *Presence in the Postmodern World*, offers a helpful examination of this change in Ellul's corpus.

the Holy Spirit,' what would the prayer that the Holy Spirit be given to us signify?)[44] And as long as He isn't there, the Word is silent. The Holy Spirit is a force that comes and goes[45] and human beings can remain in spiritual silence—the desert of the Night and silence, 'such as certain writers have described it. Think' of *The Exile of the Word*, by Neher, or of the poem by St. John of the Cross, *Obscure Night*.[46] This spiritual wilderness can last for a whole lifetime, 'imposing on someone' an absolute solitude and the temptation to despair (Kierkegaard).[47]

d. At this point, the desert is the incitement to Hope. In fact, Hope only occurs when, on the one hand, there is no human means to assure our personal future (there is no reason to hope), and on the other hand, there is no longer any personal relationship with God, no longer an immediate and present presence (the opposite being a fullness, and "can one still hope for what one sees?"[48])

Hope is the affirmation that everything remains true, even if nothing confirms it for me. It is the response of individuals—on the one hand to God's past promise, and on the other to the current silence of God ("Why have you abandoned me?")[49]—declaring that the promise remains true even if at the present time God no longer manifests it. Declaring that God remains faithful even if nothing permits me to see it today. That the Word remains objectively the word, even if I am no longer receiving it today, in my concrete life, brought up to date. That prayer is heard even if it is not answered the way I would like it to be. And it is this act of Hope, which, before God, demonstrates my faith, and before people, attests to the truth.

44. J-P.Q. Cf. Luke 11:13.

45. J-P.Q. Cf. John 3:8.

46. J-P.Q. St. John of the Cross, *Dark Night of the Soul.*

47. J-P.Q. Kierkegaard, *Sickness unto Death*, 108, 109, 111–12.

48. J-P.Q. Cf. Rom 8:24.

49. J-P.Q. Ps 22: 2; Matt 27:46; Mark 15:34. Ellul identifies the "loud cry" of Jesus on the cross with "the last temptation [which] is the temptation of despair" (Ellul, *If You Are the Son of God*, 50–52). Cf. art. "My God, my God, why have you abandoned me?" in Ellul, *Prayer and Modern Man*, 153; Ellul, *Apocalypse*, 58; Ellul, *Hope in Time of Abandonment*, 119–22; Ellul, *Anarchy and Christianity*, 83.

e. Secondly, the spiritual desert is the experience of our freedom.[50] It is a freedom that consists of : (i) being unpreoccupied with and unfocused on the self: the spiritual wilderness is only serious if I consider my experience to be more important than all else, and freedom begins with this preoccupation; (ii) being responsible in relation to what one does, that is, capable of making one's own decisions: (iii) keeping the commandments which are signs of freedom.

'Christians are individuals' who are freed and emancipated, but not at all to become slaves or robots of God. We are not neutral instruments because we have to assume our own responsibilities and act on our own (cf. the People of Israel in the desert). The "freedom" of those who have been emancipated implies precisely that God does not dictate one's will but that, in relation to our experience of being freed, we must choose and decide the path of our life. The presence of God is symbolic (such as the pillar of fire) and becomes a calling to an obedience that is freely decided upon to a word that we must reinterpret, even if we do not understand it. The spiritual wilderness is the place of our freedom, and the fact that the commandments were given in the wilderness is very significant: they are the objective limits of the possibility of living.[51]

IV. The Theological Desert

A. Theology in the Desert—The desert is not only about spiritual and emotional experiences, for on the intellectual level, theology is also related to the desert. That is to say that two theological paths 'exist today': one which functions through philosophy, knowledge, and structures created by human means (coincidence, reason/revelation, matter/grace)—and another theology devoid of all that.

50. J-P.Q. For the development of the relationship between freedom, hope, and prayer (three subjects dealt with in this paragraph and the two preceding ones), see the section titled "The Assertion of Freedom" in Ellul, *Prayer and Modern Man*, 120–39, and "Freedom" in Ellul, *Hope in Time of Abandonment*, 239–32.

51. J-P.Q. Cf. Ellul, *Unjust God*, 18: "When God gives Israel His Law at Sinai, it is just before the engagement in the desert, but it is also, at the moment the Jews become free, because they need a law so that liberty does not become incoherence and 'so that it is still possible for man to live.'"

a. We are then dealing with negative theology: if God is really God, we cannot know or say anything about him (meaning the theology of the Desert Fathers is not good: they say a lot!). God is the Totally Other 'towards whom we cannot establish' any access. We can only grasp that which God is not. And in the center remains the inexpressible and the incomprehensible. 'This theology is' tied to a nominalist stance: we must name realities we never encounter. However, God is never more than an (arbitrary) name. "Whatever" or "whomever" we call "God" cannot correspond to any representation on our part. It is a word and only that (for the linguistic reality is unpronounceable). *But,* contrary to Catholic theological rationalism, negative theology is not a theology of absence, of non-existence: it is not because we cannot rise up to heaven by our intellect that we know nothing. For even if we understand nothing of God, God remains the one who reveals himself. But the revelation is unutterable. The communication isn't from us to him, but from him to us.[52] And he is all the more authentically God in that he is hidden. He does not reveal himself except as the hidden God, and no speculation is possible from that point onward.

b. And this is connected to the Theology of the Death of God. Such a designation is absurd if it means man decrees that he has killed God, but it becomes proper if it means a calling into question of our traditional representations of God (by the critique of the incompatibility of all theology). But then 'one must seize' the important difference 'between this particular theory of the death of God and that of the death of God as Father'—for saying "it is no longer possible to call God Father because of psychoanalysis, or [illegible word][53] because of Democracy," is not the same process as putting into question the Good Lord, Providence, or the Cause of All Causes, the latter bringing us back to the question, "What is revelation itself and what are intellectual images?" Here we enter into a wilderness that man makes for himself: the hermeneutic wilderness, or wilderness of demythologizing. In other words, we turn Revelation itself into a wilderness, we create the wilderness of the Word—a place which becomes, 'as we defined it at the beginning of this study,' *yeshimon*, 'the solitude of a ravaged country,' and not *midbar*, the solitude where the

52. M.M. Ellul elaborates on this in *Living Faith*, 141–48, suggesting that human religion moves upward, whereas God's self-revelation moves downward.

53. J-P.Q. This word in its original handwritten form is illegible.

word—*davar* can be revealed. Such a theology would be correct if it led to the stripping away of every concept of God and the questioning of our discourse, if it backed us into a corner, suppressing God as a Means or Facilitator, or if it suppressed that which is Religious. But 'the fact is that' it truly situates us in a theological wilderness.

c. 'We find a good example of such a theology in the' exemplary books of Vahanian [for whom the Church regains its characteristic of being a holy people, its specific role as a people of witness (constituted but not established), and its solitude when it once again takes its God seriously as Transcendent and thinks of everything in terms of the Eschaton. That is what places it in the wilderness—the theological wilderness of Transcendence and otherness.][54] In his works we learn that, as in the wilderness, man (in himself and not the society or the sociological factor) becomes "the condition of God."[55] Both the end of the world and its origin derive from eschatology. It is not necessary that the world has meaning in itself for the glory of God to appear there. It is not God that is the condition of everything that exists, but rather, everything that exists is the condition. That of which human reality is proof is neither the proof of the presence or absence of God, but the proof of his otherness.[56] This corresponds to the New Testament: humanity has no other access to God except through Jesus, who is the human condition of Christ, the condition of the reality of God. This implies overthrowing idols,[57] in particular the idol God becomes as soon as we make the world or man depend on him, as a universal principle of application.

Thus, the Theological Wilderness implies renouncing all explanations of God derived from the Incarnation: it corresponds to the wilderness that Jesus himself experienced.

54. J-P.Q. Notes from a separate folio referring to this paragraph.

55. J-P.Q. Title of a book by Gabriel Vahanian, published in 1970 by Éditions du Seuil, often mentioned by Ellul. See, for example, Ellul, *Humiliation of the Word*, 179; Ellul, *Living Faith*, 44–45, 152–55; Ellul, *If You Are the Son of God*, 70.

56. J-P.Q. Note from a separate folio referring to this paragraph: "The possible relationship with God is not one of identity or ignorance but of otherness. . . . God is always other than that which we have determined."

57. J-P.Q. Cf. Vahanian, *Wait Without Idols*.

B. The Ethics of the Desert—Several ethical consequences 'derive from what precedes':

1. Criticism and Iconoclasm. From the moment that the idol "God" is eliminated, the destruction of everything that can have a substitutionary religious form in the world begins. Christian iconoclasm is inevitable if we take updated eschatology seriously. It is the dimension that does not tolerate any religion. And, in reality, it is also the meaning of the desert for Israel: the stripping away of all religions (hence, the prophets who always refer to the desert as the place of faithfulness).[58]

2. Worship. From the moment that we stop trying to understand this God and to build a coherent theology, the only possible relationship is worship. There again, there is a correspondence to the biblical desert: the Hebrews ask to leave for the desert to worship a god about whom they can say nothing. Worship is therefore the humbling of the mind, knowledge, philosophy . . . Entering into worship becomes the opening of self to the one whom we recognize without knowing.

3. The Choice of Powerlessness.[59] Because the wilderness is the abandonment of means, the theological wilderness is the abandonment of power in whatever form it appears (according to the results of criticism and worship). This corresponds to Israel's permanent experience with, for example, the book of Judges and the experience of Gideon. God is the one who causes us to live without means. We can see in that the extreme criticism of Technology[60] whether it be in our personal and professional

58. J-P.Q. Cf. Vahanian, *Death of God*, 58: "When the Children of Israel were settled in Canaan, the prophets kept reminding them of the unique experience they had lived through in the desert. What they meant was not a return to the social and cultural conditions of desert life, but that, *mutatis mutandis*, Israel should live in the spirit of faith in the true God which had enlivened it."

M.M. Also published earlier in 1957 by George Braziller and published and translated in 1962 by Buchet-Chastel with the title *La Mort de Dieu*.

59. M.M. Ellul distinguishes between what I would call situational and chosen powerlessness. Situational powerlessness means one has little to no power. Chosen powerlessness means one can generate and/or exercise power but decides not to. Ellul's ethics of powerlessness/non-power is derived from the latter kind. See Ellul, "Power of Technique," 242–47. For a lengthier, though untranslated, treatment of this ethic of non-power, see Ellul, *Théologie et Technique*.

60. J-P.Q. "La Technique" in French.

lives or in our collective living (where the refusal of national power, growth, and militarism 'must be affirmed').

4. Holiness. It is in the desert that the people of Israel are holy, that is, set apart. The theological wilderness is the distance in regard to all other beliefs and religions, the refusal to confuse God with some other 'god,' but also the refusal to politicize, to communize the revelation, to add "AND . . ."

5. Wisdom. [Thus, the Bible teaches us, through the Desert, a reality valid for every individual, but inacceptable for the individual, a wisdom beyond wisdoms—and we are able to receive 'this reality and this wisdom' 'only' through the Revelation of the Holy Spirit.][61] The wilderness is the expression of this fundamental reality that *if* man wants to remain or become man, *if* history has to be possible, *if* humans as a group are necessary, *if* truth must be lived, man must not accept *too much* happiness ('happiness cannot nor should not be' a total, definitive happiness) nor *too much* order. The excessive 'happiness of our time is' drugs, 'the search for' the excitement of each of the zones of the brain to produce joy, calmness, peace (*cf.* the experiments of José Delgado).[62] The excess of order is 'minimal' entropy, 'that is, the absence of life. Nothing of all that is the' truth of man, which resides in the permanent dialectic of hardship overcome, of disorder requiring reorganization: it is the very lesson of the desert, of the obliteration of the past, of chaos, of total calling into question.[63]

61. J-P.Q. Separate folio referring to this paragraph.

62. J-P.Q. José Delgado (1915–2011) is a neurophysiologist who realized from 1950 onward the first cerebral implants in animals and then in men. Cf. Ellul, *Technological System*, 258–59: "We are on the point of being able to manipulate, genetically, chemically, and *electrically* the exact human being that we want, but we really don't know what we want." See also, Ellul, *Ce Que Je Crois*, 184.

63. J-P.Q. and M.M. The conclusion of this study echoes Ellul, *Ethics of Freedom*, 301, which highlights the incompatibility between liberty in Christ and the quest in our society for order with the "network of assurances, forecasts, securities, and reciprocities" on top of "well-being . . . comfort, and happiness." A radical choice flows from that "either to stay enslaved in a life that is peaceful, assured, and comfortable, or to become free, but in the desert. No other place is compatible with liberty. . . . No other place than that which is the destruction of all guarantees, of all security, of all protection, of all order. Liberty sends us, in fact, into a desert that we must inhabit, arrange, humanize, fill with our presence. . . . To receive this calling is to accept to live in this desert, effectively putting into doubt all society's forms of security." See also the section "Happiness and Conquest," in Ellul, *Ethics of Freedom*, 258–70.

Supplementary Note[64]

The third lesson of the *Leçons sur la théologie de la liberté chrétienne* (*Lessons on the Theology of Christian Liberty*) deals with God as liberator in the Old Testament.[65] For three examples of the second part of this lesson, Jacques Ellul goes to some lengths to explain the tie between the desert and the liberation given by God.

The following is his commentary on Abraham:

> God calls him out of the city. He frees him from his riches and his security, but also, of course, from the facility of his life. The whole story of Abraham is the story of this liberation. 'Beginning' with the move into the desert 'viewed as' the place of complete liberty, the return to ground zero, that is, the new beginning of Adam, the place of the only guarantee given by God, and of the meeting with Satanic power. 'The story of Abraham allows him to experience':
>
> - Freedom from economic conditions for success—'as shown by' the dividing of the lands 'between Lot and Abraham': Abraham is not made to succeed economically and become rich. But that is only seen to the degree to which he doesn't compete with Lot and accepts the situation of a free man which means a man released from determining factors by God's previous action.[66]
> - Freedom from physiological conditions 'which bring old age into conflict' with childbearing. 'And it should be noted that Abraham' falls back into determinism when he wants to ensure by his own means that he has a descendance.[67]
> - Freedom from emotional conditions 'with' the sacrifice of 'the son agreed upon' by the father.[68]
> - Freedom from the fear of God 'with' discussion being the very essence of the prayer with God.[69]

64. K.H. Further reflections by Ellul presented by Jean-Philippe Qadri, editor of the French edition containing the text on "The Desert," in Ellul, *Vivre et penser la liberté*.

65. M.M. "Leçons sur la théologie de la liberté chrétienne," in Ellul, *Vivre et penser la liberté*, 421–43.

66. J-P.Q. Cf. Gen 13.

67. J-P.Q. Cf. Gen 16:1–6.

68. J-P.Q. Cf. Gen 22.

69. J-P.Q. Cf. Gen 18:22–33.

- Freedom even from finding a means for the realization of the promises of God; that is to say that Abraham goes back to the freedom of the decision of God, because he himself is free for the realization of the promise, both of a descendance ('which he proves by 'agreeing to' the sacrifice) and of the land (he will own no more than a tomb).[70]

Thus, Abraham experiences successive liberations, which one could consider as deprivations that translate into successes (which may be material). These successes are never the result of economic logic or power struggles, but of an unforeseeable factor, a component of freedom: freedom is not logical.

In this whole story God expresses his freedom by grace: it is free [without cost], which in reality is freedom, because it is not determined, not the result of a motive. And this state of being free is shown in a relationship of giving which is found in the ethic of freedom.[71]

The commentary on Israel in the desert (cf. supra I.II.5) highlights the terrible price of liberation and develops the concept of the Law, according to Barth:

> On the one hand Exodus shows that freedom is costly: 'its price' is the pain, evil, and suffering that falls on Egypt;[72] when the work of liberation is completed, the power of determinism, of inevitability, is paid for by man. Liberation is never a romance; it is the result of man sinking into evil. On the other hand, the people who are set free are sent into the desert: they do not enter into an easy or happy life either. In fact, the whole Old Testament establishes a contradiction between happiness and freedom.[73] The liberated people is liberated from the ease of determinism. They live day by day. They follow a guide who does not make his intentions clear. They experience an adventure which is continually renewed, that is, a daily freedom, for they continuously fall back into their desire for security (which is a desire for repetition, hence determination). And then there is the meeting with the God who gives a law; this

70. J-P.Q. Cf. Gen 23; 25:8–10.

71. J-P.Q. LTLC ("Leçons sur la théologie de la liberté chrétienne"), ff. 7–8.

72. J-P.Q. Cf. Exod 7–15.

73. J-P.Q. Cf. Ellul, *Métamorphose du bourgeois*, 160, which castigates the "imposture of claiming to hold together in the same cluster contradictory realities (such as Happiness and Liberty) because verbal confusion has permitted the coupling of the smoke with the wind."

> law in the Sinai is not a duty, an obligation, a rule for life: it traces the domain in which our liberty is situated and evolves (K. Barth).
>
> It is the test of our liberty. But every transgression is the expression of our non-liberty and enters into the domain of determination and fatality: "If you do not steal, it is because you are free from covetousness, pleasure-seeking, greed, etc. If you do not kill, it is that you are free from hatred, from violence. . . But if you come to the point of killing, you prove that you are a slave of your passions, of your motives. And at the same time, you enter into the infernal circle of violence and vengeance that one cannot break."
>
> Such is the meaning of the Law ('which reveals itself, according to Jacques Ellul,' to be "the law of liberty.") But the proof of the terrible weight of our determinations is to have transformed this law into constraints and duties.[74]

The third example, that of the Levites, called to constitute a "free people" and to be an "element of challenge to the institution" is very short-lived, and only serves to introduce the role of the prophets with the particular figure of Elijah (cf. supra I.II.7):

> The prophets pick up the task of the Levites when the latter become totally conformist, that is to say, once they have given in to fatality. The prophets are the bearers of freedom in regard to another institutionalization: that of the Royalty and the Priesthood. This shows, in fact, another side of God's work: God accepts that in the concrete conditions man has given himself, he cannot do without institutions; but this is always a factor of fatality. So God introduces in opposition to or inside the institution the bearer of its liberty, the witness who is himself free and whose life is an expression of his word, which is the Word of God.[75] 'The prophets

74. J-P.Q. LTLC, ff. 8–9.

75. J-P.Q. Today, Christians have the same role in society as Moses and the prophets had in relation to the people of Israel. "If I am sure of the coming of the Messiah, I should do everything I can so that this return be possible and happy. Therefore, I should strengthen the faith of those around me—but also show the meaning of this Kingdom in my life. It has much less to do with a political organization, in fact, than the full and complete liberation of all of humanity. God created humans free. He will create them free again. In this faith, I must show myself to be a bearer of liberty here and now. . . . It is therefore the working out of a free life, truly *free* (not meaning "liberal" or anti-conformist!), which implies a kind of struggle with the world in which we live" (Ellul, "De l'inertie au combat," 94. Because "the Scripture tells us on several occasions that we are the bearers of Christ . . . in the social or political milieu where we are called to live, we are therefore bearers of freedom directly, not only examples or signs, but effectively bearers of real liberty—with, let us not forget, the terrible responsibility that implies!"

bring to the heart of the people' the ontological challenge expressing the liberty of the Spirit of God.

Elijah is the perfect example of this freedom. It is in a state of freedom from material conditions that he hides himself in the wilderness;[76] it is in a state of freedom from political power that he comes against Ahab;[77] it is in a state of freedom from nationalism that he anoints the king of Syria.[78] But Elijah is also the bearer of the heavy price of freedom by being the instigator of the massacre of the priests of Baal (a massacre parallel 'to that of the first-born' of Egypt).[79] For one should not mix up love with the weakness that leads to accepting the triumph of alienating powers—and that which embodies these powers can be condemned (historically, but not in eternity).

Following that, all the prophets are bearers of the same testimony and of the identification of freedom with the liberty of the Spirit of God. But they, too, will be absorbed by fatality. Thus, God acts with supreme freedom 'in the person of' Jesus Christ.[80]

Bibliography

Ballanfat, Paul. "Genies." In *Dictionnaire du Coran*, edited by Mohammad Ali Amir-Moezzi. Paris: Robert Laffont Bouqins, 2007.

Ellul, Jacques. *Anarchy and Christianity*. Translated by Geoffrey W. Bromiley. Eugene, OR: Wipf & Stock, 1991.

———. *Apocalypse: The Book of Revelation*. Translated by George W. Schreiner. New York: Seabury, 1975.

———. *Ce Que Je Crois*. Paris: Grasset, 1987.

Ellul, *Ethics of Freedom*, 399). Furthermore, "Christians are called to be bearers of liberty in this society where technical conditioning is more and more rigorous, more and more determinative for human beings" (Ellul, *Ellul par lui-même*, 161). See also Ellul and Garrigou-Lagrange, *À temps et à contretemps*, 74. On the level of nations, Ellul affirms that "if the Jewish people often appeared to us as a hard kernel, impossible to assimilate," it is because they were the "guardians of the freedom given by God," refusing "the temptation to let themselves be assimilated by societies where people confused freedom with laxism"; and still in "our day" (in 1990), "despite the army, the police, the Mossad, and everything else," "Israel is the only bearer of liberty" from "Israël, inventeur de la liberté" (Ellul, *Israël, chance de civilisation*, 247).

76. J-P.Q. 1 Kgs 19:4–8.

77. J-P.Q. 1 Kgs 18:16–19; 21:17–24.

78. J-P.Q. 1 Kgs 19:15.

79. J-P.Q. J-P.Q. 1 Kgs 18:40.

80. J-P.Q. LTLC, f° 9.

———. "De l'inertie au combat." In *La patience—Passion de la durée consentie*, edited by Catherine Chalier, 90–97. Paris: Autrement, 1992.
———. *Ellul par lui-même*. Edited by Willem Vanderburg. Paris: Editions de la Table Ronde, 2008.
———. *The Ethics of Freedom*. Translated by Geoffrey W. Bromiley. London: Mowbrays, 1976.
———. *Hope in Time of Abandonment*. Translated by C. Edward Hopkin. Eugene, OR: Wipf & Stock, 1973.
———. *The Humiliation of the Word*. Translated by Joyce Main Hanks. Grand Rapids: Eerdmans, 1985.
———. *If You Are the Son of God: The Suffering and Temptations of Jesus*. Translated by Anne-Marie Andreasson-Hogg. Eugene, OR: Cascade, 2014.
———. *Israël, chance de civilization*. France: Premiere Partie, 2008.
———. *Living Faith*. Translated by Peter Heinegg. Eugene, OR: Wipf & Stock, 1983.
———. *La Métamorphose du bourgeois*. Paris: Table Ronde, 1998.
———. *The New Demons*. Translated by C. Edward Hopkin. New York: Seabury, 1975.
———. *On Freedom, Love, and Power*. Translated by Willem H. Vanderburg. Toronto: University of Toronto Press, 2010.
———. "The Power of Technique and the Ethics of Non-Power." In *The Myths of Information: Technology and Postindustrial Culture*, translated by Mary Lydon, 242–47. Madison, WI: Coda, 1980.
———. *Prayer and Modern Man*. Translated by C. Edward Hopkin. New York: Seabury, 1970.
———. *The Technological System*. Translated by Joachim Neugroschel. New York: Continuum, 1977.
———. *Théologie et Technique*. Edited by Yves Ellul and Frédéric Rognon. Beauregard: Labor et Fides, 2014.
———. *To Will and To Do*. Translated by C. Edward Hopkin. Boston: Pilgrim, 1969.
———. *An Unjust God? A Christian Theology of Israel in Light of Romans 9–11*. Translated by Anne-Marie Andreasson-Hogg. Eugene, OR: Cascade, 2012.
———. *Vivre et penser la liberté*. Edited by Jean-Philippe Qadri. Geneva: Labor et Fides, 2019.
Ellul, Jacques, and Madeline Garrigou-Lagrange. *À temps et à contretemps*. Paris: Le Centurion, 1981.
Kierkegaard, Søren. *The Sickness unto Death*. Translated by Howard and Edna Hong. Princeton: Princeton University Press, 1980.
Rollison, Jacob Marques. *A New Reading of Jacques Ellul: Presence and Communication in the Postmodern World*. Lanham, MD: Lexington, 2020.
St. John of the Cross. "The Dark Night of the Soul." https://www.poetryfoundation.org/poems/157984/the-dark-night-of-the-soul.
Le Trésor de la Langue Française informatisé. http://atilf.atilf.fr/.
Vahanian, Gabriel. *The Death of God*. Eugene, OR: Wipf & Stock, 2009.
———. *Wait Without Idols*. New York: Braziller, 1964.

Chapter Two

The Man-Made[1] Wasteland

A Cartography

AMY ERICKSON

Introduction

DURING THE COVID-19 PANDEMIC, a large American church asked a staff member to deliver the prayer of the people in a prerecorded worship service. A white police officer had recently killed George Floyd, and the country was roiling in the painful re-exposure of deeply ingrained racial injustice. Outrage and grief compounded with the restlessness, uncertainty, and strain brought on by months of social distancing. Sensitive to these complicating currents and wanting to voice a sincere, true, and gracious petition in response, the staff member decided to rely on the Holy Spirit's guidance in the moment of prayer instead of on a premeditated script. When the time came for the recording session, they felt the Spirit's outpoured provision of words and inspiration. It was an unrepeatable gift, the type one may receive and share, but not conceal and redraw as one handles a gun. When the prayer finished, the videographer asked to reshoot the recording. The lighting was not right.

Forty years earlier, Jacques Ellul observed "western people no longer hear; everything is grasped by sight."[2] Even the church partakes in this col-

1. I am sensitive to the gender-inclusive problematics of the noun *man* versus *human*, which is why elsewhere in this piece I will refer to the *human-caused* as opposed to *man-made* wasteland. *Man-made* simply packs alliterative punch.

2. Ellul, *Humiliation of the Word*, 204.

lective deafness, reasoning "since people no longer understand the word, we should use propaganda: 'audiovisuals,' expositions, and large gatherings where the word will be only background noise or a pretext." Ellul concludes, "Such a gathering is an image in itself."[3] These comments, made in his defining work *Humiliation of the Word*, distill Ellul's enduring, iconoclastic critiques of modernity. Ellul's are critiques that rely on the distinction between the dynamic, elusive nature of the spoken word and the frozen, pervasive nature of the image, even in its more animated, audio-visual variations. This word-image binary joins with several others—subject and object, presence and absence, truth and reality, time and space—to form the scaffolding of Ellul's account of the modern condition in *Humiliation* and his other writings. Yet this account rests on a hidden but recently unearthed foundation that provides the subject for the volume in hand: an early paper on the desert.[4]

Ellul's desert essay remains unfinished. A middle section, sandwiched between accounts of the edifying wilderness of the Bible and the trying wilderness of spiritual experience, is itself deserted. The missing contents are only hinted at by cursory notes. In them, Ellul indicates that a significant difference exists between a human-caused wasteland and the biblical wilderness. He suggests that the Bible alludes to this human-made wasteland through the Hebrew word *yeshimon*, a less-common synonym to the much more prevalent *midbar*.[5] Yet after this brief mention of *yeshimon*, Ellul's desert essay fixates on *midbar*. Despite several unsavory aspects as a place of temptation, testing, and demonic habitation, overall *midbar* is

3. Ellul, *Humiliation of the Word*, 202.

4. In the rest of this paper I will use the word *wilderness* to designate the biblical desert and the term *wasteland* to designate the human-caused desert. Behind both is the single French word *désert*. I use these English terms to recognize what I take to be a key distinction in Ellul's own account, one which is loosely mirrored by the biblical nomenclature (see next footnote).

5. We may wonder at the artificiality of this distinction. In the Bible's characteristic parallelisms, *yeshimon* often lands in the same breath as *midbar*, suggesting that the terms bear more resemblance than difference (Deut 32:10; Ps 78:40; 106:14; 107:4; Isa 43:19–20). Elsewhere *yeshimon* functions as a place name: Jeshimon designates an area at the base of Mount Peor and Mount Pisgah (Num 21:20) near the country of Moab, southeast of the Dead Sea, where the Israelites were plagued after engaging in worship of the Moabite god Baal (Num 25; see also Josh 22:17). It was here that Balaam refused to curse the Israelites (Num 23:28), and where David hid from the murderous Saul (1 Sam 23:19, 24; 26:1, 3). Despite obvious linguistic overlaps between *yeshimon* and *midbar*, these latter stories suggest that *yeshimon* invokes the negative effects of human sin, especially envy, lust, and greed.

constructively defined as *the place where humanity is addressed by God's Word*. Hence, as Ellul notes, the shared tri-consonantal root *d-b-r* with the Hebrew *dabar* (word). The wilderness is where humanity is spoken to by God (Hosea 2:14), but what is the human-caused wasteland?

In this chapter, I complete the unfinished typology of Ellul's desert essay by defining and detailing the kind of desert brought into existence by human action. I distinguish this desert from the biblical wilderness with the name *wasteland* and show, if the biblical wilderness is where humanity is directly addressed by God's Word, then the human-made wasteland is where humans fail to address and be addressed by one another.[6] The wilderness is filled with God's Word; the wasteland is littered by failed dialogue. The human wasteland is a grand undeliverable message writ unknowingly large across the domains of human existence. It is a landscape which dominates contemporary life.

Ellul implicitly defines the human-made wasteland in this way throughout his corpus. With recourse to Ellul, other scholars, and contemporary examples, I describe how the wasteland of modernity distorts two key components of authentic communication: time and bodies. As illustrated in the opening anecdote, unfortunately the sands of this desertification already have blown into the boundaries of ecclesial existence.[7] Yet the reservoirs of the church's own doctrine and practices promise to help her resist the wasteland and to re-enter the wilderness as the place where she addresses others and is herself addressed.

The Wasteland as Failed Address

The nature, and indeed the causes, of the human-caused wasteland are not detailed in Ellul's desert essay. However, the notion—as observed in the second footnote of the newly released essay—appears in *New Demons*.[8] Ellul's guiding thesis here is that the secularization of modernity is in fact a sacralization of new domains: most of all, technique.[9] In chapter 5, "Secular

6. In this claim, this chapter harmonizes with Jacob Marques Rollison's analysis of Ellul's account of language vis à vis contemporary philosophy. See Rollison, *New Reading of Jacques Ellul*.

7. We should wonder if the crisis of actual desertification is coincidental. United Nations Convention to Combat Desertification, "United Nations Decade for Deserts."

8. Ellul, "Desert," 9.

9. See Hallowell, Review of *The New Demons*.

Religions," Ellul suggests that historical religions amount to humanity's search for a dialogue partner. In other words, religions are the track record of humanity's efforts to "people" the world with communicable powers, be they gods, spirits, angels, or demons.[10] "Except in the case of individuals," Ellul concludes, "there is no instance in which human groups have not wanted, at any cost, to populate the world by someone other than man, someone who could make answer to a continuing discourse."[11]

Today this need for a dialogue partner is painfully felt, but largely unmet. Ellul writes, "Here is man in his new milieu, in our modern society, feeling alone all over again, and without a respondent. He directs at the empty sky a discourse without dialogue. He embraces things, which are never anything but objects. He is living anew the horror of silence and incompleteness."[12] Ellul explicitly describes this existence—one which is "without dialogue"—as a human wasteland:

> Modern man in these grandiose cities, in these feverish exchanges, in the continual chatter of radio and television, knows *the human wasteland* perhaps as never before. . . . *The human wasteland* of the big city or the highway is even more disquieting and oppressive because new questions without number come to the lips of modern man and arise in his heart. There is no one to give him an answer. How can he talk with a computer? So, in this new solitude . . . man looks everywhere for someone who will tell him the truth, someone who will enter into a meaningful relationship. In so doing, he duplicates the old traditional movement. He has to people his *wasteland* with new genii and new superpowers.[13]

Ellul shows at length in *New Demons* that humanity is no less religious today than before, despite its tacit assumptions and explicit proclamation of near if not total secularization in the West. However, it is worth wondering whether humanity's zealous search for a meaningful dialogue partner has ever been more ineffective, or misplaced. T. S. Elliot's poem *The Waste Land*, which Ellul admired, also chronicles humanity's failed attempt to secure a dialogue partner in the midst of the wasteland of "urban sprawl and decay."[14] Writing in the wake of WWI and the Spanish Flu epidemic (from

10. Ellul, *New Demons*, 130.
11. Ellul, *New Demons*, 130.
12. Ellul, *New Demons*, 130.
13. Ellul, *New Demons*, 130–31; emphasis added
14. I take this phrase from correspondence with Ellul scholar Michael Morelli, who

which both Eliot and his wife suffered), Eliot's poem lacks "the stabilizing force of a central figure" and

> gives way to a polyphony of perspectives that search for revelation which is found to be unintelligible. . .The voices of the poem's prophets, the Sibyl, Madame Sosostris, and Tiresias, interweave with the lives of the waste land's inhabitants offering only riddles and silence in response to their questions. In a world of fragmentation, the knowledge of the seers is meaningless and just as incapable of expressing reality as any other visionary voice.[15]

In search of a true word, humanity encounters "only a heap of broken images."[16] Yet, longing for the tangible presence of and meaningful dialogue with another and/or an Other, their desperation for a stabilizing and comforting sense of transcendence when locked within meaningless immanent material often causes humans to fuse the fragmented images to create something, anything that might provide orientation and solace in the human-made wasteland.

The Eclipse of Coeval Time

As Ellul fervently argues throughout *Humiliation of the Word*, modernity is obsessed with images. Because of this, and despite the illusions generated by hyperactive communication, words are disregarded and humiliated. Ellul says this humiliation occurs when space takes precedence over time: sight is spatial, sound is temporal. Time—and with time, the spoken word—"inserts us within a duration rather than an expanse."[17] Looking at an image requires only a momentary glance, but it takes time to say something, just as it takes time to listen. Of course, not everything that involves words is solely based on time. Writing—and any recording for that matter—spatializes speech.[18] Both make something otherwise unrepeatable, repeatable. One can turn back a page just as one can rewind a recording. But "ask the person speaking with you to repeat the explanation he has just

drew my attention to Ellul's affinity for Eliot's poem. Personal email correspondence, June 11, 2020.

15. Picard and van Gemerden, "Theological Engagement with T. S. Eliot's Waste Land."

16. Eliot, "Waste Land."

17. Ellul, *Humiliation of the Word*, 13.

18. Ellul, *Humiliation of the Word*, 44.

given, and it will be different."[19] Consequently, for Ellul, as soon as speech becomes a written or audiovisual recording, dialogue is aborted.

Although writing is by no means a modern invention, what is unique to the modern world is the accelerated production and use—by means of technological "advances"—of spatialized speech. Just the names of today's prevailing social media and communication apps show the extensive advancement of the spatializing and visualization of communication and the ensuing diminishment of time. Instagram relays its content in an "instant," Twitter glories in staccato "tweets" over sustained and interactive discussion, as does the snappiness of Snapchat. Even Facebook ostensibly archives pictorial "faces" instead of dialogical conversation.[20] Time is contracted, because like a loafing geriatric, dilated time hinders the colonization of seemingly endless space by technology's advancements.

There are at least four ways that time is reduced at the hands of our own times: by conceptions that time is measured instead of filled, progressive instead of apocalyptic, homogenous and pervasive instead of anchored by a past and a future, and simultaneous instead of contemporaneous. All of these misconceptions—which are more than mere misconceptions, but actual distortions of time—also prevent time from being shared. This ability of time to be shared is what anthropologist Johannes Fabian terms "coevalness," which could be defined as time-full contemporaneity.[21] Only coeval time allows for true encounter and dialogue. As Willie Jennings notes, "communication is, ultimately, about creating shared Time."[22] Ellul wholeheartedly agrees, explaining that the conditions for a dialogue include "duration, two people (the speaker and the listener, who are living in the same moment of time), and concentration on the fact that the past is abolished."[23] But in the human-made wasteland, instead of allowing an encounter between subjects, time is enslaved by the circulation of objects who can neither speak to one another nor listen.

19. Ellul, *Humiliation of the Word*, 44.

20. In the rest of this piece, I will continue to use social media apps as illustrations of the dynamics of the wasteland's failed address. This is not to suggest that some sense of encounter or dialogue cannot occur through these mediums. Quite the contrary. However, their limits—and their illusions—need to be acknowledged, as well as their power in both conditioning and colonizing our habits of interaction and speech.

21. Johannes, *Time and the Other*, 30–31, cited in Jennings, *Christian Imagination*, loc. 1018.

22. Jennings, *Christian Imagination*, loc. 1018.

23. Ellul, *Humiliation of the Word*, 15.

Measured vs. Filled

In *Becoming Friends of Time*, John Swinton recounts the development of Western conceptions of time, especially as emblematized and propagated by the invention of the clock. The clock ushered in the notion that time could be measured, and by virtue of being measured, also commodified, exchanged, and controlled. The clock atomized time into seconds, minutes, and hours; it quite literally delivered time into human-made hands.[24] Time could now be *manipulated* (from Latin *manus*, hand).

Ironically, the English word *clock* derives from a word for bell, betraying its origin in the lives of monastics for whom bells signaled their daily rounds of prayer.[25] For these monks, time was not an instrument for human manipulation and production. Rather, time was the arena to faithfully encounter and worship God.[26] As put by Ephraim Radner in *A Time to Keep*, time—theologically speaking—is not "spent" in the dripping sand of seconds, but is rather offered.[27] Time, when conceived relationally instead of abstractly, is not measured but filled. Indeed, in the fullness of time God sent his Word to encounter humanity within history (Gal 4:4). Ellul notes that in the pre-technical era, humans ate when hungry and slept when sleepy.[28] Each activity was determined by its own inherent timeliness (Eccl 3:1–8), not by its maximization and efficiency.

This obsession with measuring and controlling time is perhaps no more evident than in Western church members' common complaint that a Sunday morning service has gone "too long." The Christian satirical newspaper *The Babylon Bee* mockingly relays in the faux-headline article "Church Service Goes Into Record 7th Overtime" how "The pastor continued to rack up point after point, blowing through regulation time and pushing the service into multiple overtimes before finally wrapping things up at the 74th sermon point."[29] The real butt of the joke is not the pastor who oversteps their temporal bounds but the complaining congregation. The article pointedly notes that "the Apostle Paul actually killed someone by preaching too long, and so may still hold the all-time record for the most

24. Swinton, *Becoming Friends of Time*, 22–23.

25. Swinton, *Becoming Friends of Time*, 26.

26. Swinton, *Becoming Friends of* Time, 26.

27. Radner, *Time to Keep*, 5.

28. Ellul, *Technological Society*, 325.

29. "Church Service Goes Into Record 7th Overtime."

overtimes in a service." We can dismiss the teasing jest, but it calls attention to the sobering reality that the time of the church's gathering often is counted and spent, but not shared.

Progressive vs. Apocalyptic

The measurability of time segues into another feature of modern conceptions of time: its linearity, and with this, its progression. This myth of the inevitably of human progression—also known as the myth of civilization—takes a number of forms.[30] The theory of evolution, with its broader social and economic implications, is perhaps the most familiar of these architectonic myths which order the west and joins with wider assumptions that humans developed from backward, cave-dwelling savages to advanced, technology-wielding citizens. But this popular cultural cliché hangs on deep philosophical moorings, established by Hegelianism and presumptuously showcased in Francis Fukuyama's daring claim that Western democracy is the pinnacle of political progression, and as such constitutes the "end" of history.[31]

Although the faith of the Old Testament Israelites was unique in positing historical time—as opposed to cyclical time—as the locus of theological meaning and of God's engagement with humanity, this history was not conceived as strictly linear, and certainly not as "progressive."[32] In the Bible, the events of history stand equidistant before the Day of Judgment to which they must give account (e.g., Joel 2:1, 11; Amos 5:18; Zeph 1:14). The expanse of time and Israel's location within history did not make them any less distant from this coming eschatological end. Biblically and theologically, history itself is ever in the shadow of the Apocalypse, of God's great revealing (Luke 8:17; 12:2–3). The Apocalypse is not an event which time flows towards. Instead, the Apocalypse flows towards time (Heb 10:25). The nearness of this disruption gives time its theological significance, not the flow of time itself. Nevertheless, contemporary culture insists that time "marches on." Because of this, it cannot heed those who exist within time, let alone stop to converse with them, let alone sense the presence of the ever inbreaking Apocalypse, and with it, a revelation of Israel's God.

30. See Wagenfuhr, *Plundering Eden*, 33–55.

31. Fukuyama, *End of History and the Last Man*.

32. See Eliade and Trask, *Sacred and the Profane*, 110; Anderson, *Understanding the Old Testament*, 146.

Homogenous vs. Anchored

In the wake of myths of progress, Fukuyama's aforementioned *End of History* marks entry into an estuary where the waters of progressive, linear time intermix with an ocean of homogenized time. The twentieth-century French philosopher Jean Baudrillard (favorably cited by Ellul on occasion) observes that the real issue is not that history may have come to an end, but that it may not *have* an end. That is, history may lack any *telos* or meaning.[33] One commentator notes,

> Because of its origin and ethic, Baudrillard . . . sees America as leading the way here since it was 'created in the hope of escaping from history, of building a utopia sheltered from history . . .' America is a society that has founded itself, not on a process of historical evolution as might be said of European nations, but on a set of philosophical utopian principles. Thus it undervalues both past and future in its fixation with a fantastic utopian present. 'Having known no primitive accumulation of time, it lives in a perpetual present . . .' So everywhere we are seeing the disintegration of linear time narratives [in part as the result of] *temporal acceleration*. There is an impatient immediacy about our society; objects, information, and images are all circulating at such a speed that all events are pre-empted, reduced to spectacle with predetermined outcomes.[34]

Despite the residual notions of a linear and progressive time, time today—especially in America—is decoupled from both the past and future. This results in a homogenized time with no distinct temporal inflection that can be meaningfully entered, understood, or shared. Instagram scrolls users through an endlessly suspended time frame. TikTok immerses viewers in video clips spliced together with an unknown past and unshared future. As Zygmunt Bauman observes in *Liquid Modernity*, this hyper-visualized and hyper-immediate communication exponentially allows for the meeting of strangers, which is the hallmark of city life. But this is not really a meeting, it is more a "mis-meeting"; strangers have no past or future to ground their interaction because the meetings are more transitory than extended.[35]

33. Walters, *Baudrillard and Theology*, 81.

34. Walters, *Baudrillard and Theology*, 82.

35. Bauman, *Liquid Modernity*, 95.

Simultaneity vs. Contemporaneity

Homogenized time allows its inhabitants to coordinate time in terms of simultaneity rather than contemporaneity. A word analysis may be instructive here. *Simultaneous* derives from the Latin *similis*, which means *like* (or *similar*).[36] Time, according to this definition, can be coordinated because of its *likeness*. Thus, technology users may communicate or participate in online meetings or streamed events because of their *simultaneity*. As Ellul articulates, "Audiovisual material is the reconstruction of detemporalized, dismantled reality that has been retemporalized."[37] But as Baudrillard notes, "Imagining others and everything which brings you closer to them is futile the instant that 'communication' can make their presence immediate."[38] By artificially closing the distances of space that separate communicants, supposedly synchronized forms of communication construct an artificial temporality (i.e. so-called *real time*) which eclipses the differences upon which true dialogical communication can occur.

Compare this false dismantling and reconstruction of time with the etymology of contemporaneity, literally *with time*. Contemporaries share time with one another. Their contemporaneousness grounds their communication. And, perhaps surprisingly, true contemporaries need not occupy the same historical period. Hence how Paul, through means of a letter, can conceive of himself as present with the gathered Corinthian community (1 Cor 5:3–4). In turn, it is only from a perceived sense of contemporaneousness with Paul before an awaited *eschaton* that the modern church continues to read him not as a voice from a distant past, but as a living voice. Contemporaries enjoy true relationship. Those who engage in simultaneity only coordinate with one another, but do not encounter one another. They are parallel lines who fail to converge.

The Eclipse of Bodily Gift

Time is not the only entity distorted in a manner that prevents genuine encounter and dialogue. There are at least three ways that bodies are eclipsed today in ways that prevent bodies from serving as a site and means of true address: the accelerated decoupling of bodies from speech, the anonymizing

36. Merriam-Webster Dictionary, s.v. "Simultaneous"; s.v. "Same."

37. Ellul, *Humiliation of the Word*, 140.

38. Baudrillard, *Ecstasy of Communication*, 40.

of the bodies of both speakers and addressees, and the treatment of bodies as commodities instead of gifts.

Decoupled from Speech

The body is the wellspring of speech. To produce sound, the muscles in the diaphragm contract to expel air from the lungs. This expelled air is intricately shaped into meaningful patterns by movements of the jaw, tongue, and lips. Sign language is no less bodily of course; hands do the linguistic grunt work instead of the mouth. For both sign language and spoken language, live speech is heavily inflected by non-verbal communication. Posture, gestures, facial expression, and tone all mingle with spoken and gestured words to communicate between bodies. Indeed, a person's brain, gut, heart, and spirit generate and shape what it is they have to say. The whole body is an instrument of speech.

Written forms of discourse, as Ellul highlights, relocate live speech from the medium of time into linear space. They also relocate speech from its immediate source in the body to an external venue. But this does not dethrone the body as the originating source of communication. Fingers must still push pens to form written words, or finger keyboards to type them. (Likewise, those who are differently abled utilize other means of extracting meaning from the body's movements by way of gesture or dictation machines and similar technologies.) Simultaneous means of communication must deconstruct and replicate acoustic waves over the phone to mimic speech or arrange pixels to mirror bodily gestures through a screen. These latter forms are simulacra of unmediated address. As any Zoom-fatigued communicant knows, they are only an ersatz replacement for embodied dialogue.[39]

The decoupling of speech from bodies is no newcomer on the stage of human history, but the extension and exacerbation of this decoupling has been uniquely accelerated by technical means. These same means also erase the distance they create. Pictures of correspondents in texting or social media apps such as Facebook reclaim the illusion that one is communicating more directly with an actual human body than employing another medium. Old-fashioned letters create no such illusion. The letter-reader is solely in the presence of the letter, not a simulation of the person who penned it. Yet fascinatingly, the very dimensions of texts—up until their proliferation

39. Jiang, "The Reason Zoom Calls Drain Your Energy."

in minisculized social media forms—were proportional to the dimensions of the human body.[40] Older forms of communication displayed a bodily awareness which is today lacking.

Thus, speech has existed apart from their originating bodies for some time. But what is unique today is not only the ease with which this separation is made possible, but the degree to which it is masked. Bodies become something to be seen or staged, as given in this chapter's opening example. (It was the lighting that mattered, not the person giving voice to prayer.) The individual body and the person it identified mattered less than the presentation. For, to be seen and heard, the body in the camera's frame apparently had to be seen and heard in a particular kind of light, otherwise it would not be seen and heard at all. Consequently, bodies in these contexts are not conceived as housing a person to be encountered and attentively seen and heard. Rather, they are perceived and treated as bodies requiring direction for the purposes of performance.

Anonymizing of Speakers and Addressees

The decoupling of the body of the speaker from the artefact of their speech allows for their anonymizing. Well known today is the internet troll who, safely shielded by their screen and wholly unidentifiable by their online identity, lobs harmful and shameful comments at people that they would cower if required to deliver them in person. Their anonymity deflects responsibility in the truest sense of the word because they are not obligated to give an account for their inflammatory speech. Anonymous speech divorces the author's body from the body of their text. In so doing, it precludes any direct response from the reader, who does not know to whom a response should be directed.

Brian Brock, writing on Kierkegaard, examines with the Danish philosopher the "pleasures of the impersonal" which constitute the "lure of anonymity."[41] The forces of speed and emotivism which heighten the lure of anonymity tend "to produce [individuals that Kierkegaard] believed to be capable only of what he called 'dribbling performances' that might look

40. Bringhurst, *Elements of Typographic Style.*

41. Though to be fair, Brock notes how Kierkegaard's own wielding of pseudonyms leveraged anonymity to race towards empathy with others as a tool for inhabiting their perspectives and desires. Brock, "Kierkegaard, Theology, and the Information Society," 457.

good in 140 characters but could not stand deeper interrogation."[42] The habits of anonymized speech, compounded with the eclipse of time examined above, encourages language that sensationally attracts a hearing for a short moment. But these communicative habits do not cultivate language that can withstand the forces of time and personal attention which are requisite for a meaningful dialogue to occur.

The anonymizing of speakers has a close cousin: the anonymizing of those spoken to. These do not always coincide. The anonymized internet troll (usually) knows exactly at whom they are hurling their insults; conversely, the named owner of a social media account—or YouTube channel, or church website on which services are livestreamed—largely speaks to an anonymous audience. Even those who broadcast their social media posts to a designated subset of family and friends rarely address anyone in particular. When speech is shaped to reach a mass instead of an individual, the content of that speech is indelibly altered.

When broadcasted to instead of addressed, people are not spoken to for their edification, or literally, their building up. Instead, they are spoken to for the building of the platform for which they serve as consumers. Church services—whether online or in-person—are often no less guilty than the individual social media account wielder in this regard. Worship service numbers and online users are just that: *useful* for adding to a numerical count that serves to validate the ministry producing content to be consumed, rather than a word to be heard—and returned in kind.[43]

Ellul insists that such broadcasted speech is inherently unchristian. In our age, he writes, speaking

> is anything at all except saying *something* to *someone*. . . . Language has become anything at all: a social adapter, an instrument of control and conformity, a signal, ideological reproduction, a framework, alienation of the speaker, etc. It has become anything at all, but never the creative source of meaning; it is never a word borne by a human being and therefore a human word.[44]

Communication today is noisy and unconstructive to the same extent that it only values the persons who receive it as serving to uptick a numerical count, not as possessors of a distinct and unique body and voice, with its attendant unique desires, stories, and possible reply. Indeed, any language

42. Brock, "Kierkegaard, Theology, and the Information Society," 455.

43. Benjamin, *Race after Technology*, 13.

44. Ellul, *Humiliation of the Word*, 172.

unfueled by love is but a clanging cymbal (1 Cor 13:1). So often today we speak not to be of use to the one spoken to, but to use the listener for the sake of our speech. Dialogue becomes impossible because it is not in service to a real and living relationship.

Commodities vs. Gifts

The separation of speech and bodies through the anonymization of both speaker and listener culminates in a distorted view of bodies themselves. Bodies are perceived as products for consumption instead of artefacts of eloquence; they are handled as commodities rather than given as gifts.

Ellul notes how Adam bursts into speech when presented with the body of Eve because he perceives both difference (gender) and similarity (humanity) between them. This dialectic of difference and similarity is a necessary ingredient for dialogue:

> I do not speak to a person identical to me. I must have something to say which the other lacks, but he must also be different from me. Yet similarity is required as well. . . . Speech fills the infinite gap that separates us. But the difference is never removed. Discourse begins again and again because the distance between us remains.[45]

The view of another body—perceptively similar, yet different—prompts Adam to speak both *because of* Eve and *for* Eve.[46] Awareness of the otherness of another's body gives rise to true speech with them.

The body serves as the visible manifestation of a concrete, unique, unrepeatable person. It makes externally visible the fact that there is an individual to speak with; they offer a "you" to whom address can be directed. At the same time, our bodies also make it evident that there is an individual "I" to whom is tethered a unique perspective from which they may speak.[47] As John Paul II observes, we tend to think of communication today in terms of the media that relay them. But we forget that the originating "media" are bodies themselves, since "through its own visibility, the body *manifests* man and, in manifesting him, acts as an intermediary that allows man and woman, from the beginning, to 'communicate' with each

45. Ellul, *Humiliation of the Word*, 17.

46. Ellul, *Humiliation of the Word*, 17. See John Paul II, *Man and Woman He Created Them*, 161.

47. John Paul II, *Man and Woman He Created Them*, 176.

other."[48] Modern modes of communication often choke dialogue because they frequently remain blind to the relation between communicants and their bodies. Today we substitute an "I-Thou" relationship for an "I-It" one.[49] Bodies are objects, not subjects, as evident in two highly charged domains: race and sex.

Willie Jennings' writings unmask how early colonizers measured the world for development and profitability by evaluating human bodies according to a scale of whiteness.[50] Unreflective colonialists and even well-meaning Christians installed a "vision of a world that revolves around a centered White self, a body that projects meaning onto the world . . . in order to bring nature and human beings to maturity, to the full realization of their purpose and their *use*."[51] Whiteness evaluates bodies—human, animal, and territorial—by their potential for profitability rather than intimacy. Bodies, in this white gaze, are not subjects of eloquence but objects for use.

In her book *Race after Technology*, Ruha Benjamin hauntingly illustrates how technology, far from serving as a neutral arbiter, is sinisterly encoded by this racist outlook. Technology is programmed with the racist views of its programmers. Benjamin calls this "the New Jim Code," a phenomenon which augments and buries racism in "layers of digital denial."[52] As Benjamin compellingly suggests, race is itself a technology, used to subjugate and stratify people through one-dimensional stereotypes and litmus tests of categorization that enable them to be bought, sold, and marketed.[53] These technological "developments" are considered inevitable stages of progress. Yet we fail to acknowledge that society shapes the technology it is in turn shaped by, while turning a blind eye to the racial input which feeds the racial output of our technologies.[54] This lack of responsibility underscores that bodies themselves do not take part in the free, responsive exchange of genuine dialogue. Rather, technological surveillance of bodies programmatically gazes at bodies, but refuses to listen to them.

48. John Paul II, *Man and Woman He Created Them*, 176.

49. Buber, *I and Thou*.

50. Sechrest et al., *Can "White" People Be Saved?*, 137.

51. Sechrest et al., *Can "White" People Be Saved?*, 137; emphasis added.

52. Benjamin, *Race after Technology*, 12.

53. Benjamin, *Race after Technology*, 21, 36.

54. Benjamin, *Race after Technology*, 39–40.

Race is not the only domain in which bodies suffer from commodification. So is sex, and sexuality. The popular linguistic coinage of "heterosexual" and "homosexual" and consequential smorgasbord of sexualities that continue to proliferate insist on inscribing and identifying one's body by the subset of bodies deemed to possess maximum potential for one's own sexual gratification. Bodies are not identified as gifts to be given over to another in all their vexing and impenetrable concreteness, but as a locus of consumption and penetration determined by ever-more granular typologies. In this way, identity is constructed on a scale of objectification of other bodies.

But these are not the only objects for consumption; one's *own* body is presented as a product for sale on a competitive market for sexualized attention. Jean Baudrillard's assessment of modern society as a circulation and "system of objects" instead of an arena of dialectically engaged subjects is compelling here. He identifies the body as the central object of this system, in which "the sexually attractive body is the competitive consumer object which has maximized its capital."[55] It is no surprise, then, that plastic surgery has become a popular procedure to advance one's bodily capital in the market of sexual attention.

Through both racialized and sexualized constructions, our age views and values bodies as products instead of gifts, as objects instead of subjects.[56] Bodies are the sites of exploitation and seduction instead of instruments of dialogue. By contrast, John Paul II, in his intricate analysis of the creation account, observes that theologically, the human body is a sign of "creative donation."[57] The human body is the primal witness to the unbidden and unearned gift that is creation. Human bodies themselves exist—as Adam becomes aware by the presentation of Eve—*with* another as well as *for* another. As with any gift, the body establishes three things: the one who gives, the one who receives, and the relationship between them.[58] Our inability of conceiving and receiving each other's bodies as gifts, rather than as commodities or as consumers, perpetuates our inability to truly speak to and be addressed by one another in genuine intercourse.

55. Walters, *Baudrillard and Theology*, 108.

56. "The subjectivity of the person gives way in some sense to the objectivity of the body." John Paul II, *Man and Woman He Created Them*, 259.

57. John Paul II, *Man and Woman He Created Them*, 183.

58. John Paul II, *Man and Woman He Created Them*, 180.

Altogether, our age is one that distorts time and bodies. Genuine dialogue between persons withers as a direct result. We fragment and reassemble our potential dialogue partners into quantifiable, collectable, and exchangeable units that contain no unique qualities and therefore demand neither unique attention nor speech. By abstracting communication from both time and bodies, our contemporary age does not deal with "living words," enfleshed words, which are the gospel's true form.[59] Instead, by stripping language from particular times and particular bodies, we deny its humble and powerful corporeality. As a result, much of what passes for communication today is a "talking at" rather than a "speaking with." Our attempts at address, suspended in commodified time between commodified bodies, are broadcast widely across the wasteland of our existence. Yet, they take no root and bear no fruit in the nutrient-depleted ground of this land.

Ecclesial Reservoirs

I have devoted most of the allotted space of this chapter to a cartography of the wasteland of our era, highlighting some of the defining features that suggest it is a desert which fails to generate space and time for genuine dialogue between human creatures. I have indicated, too, that the church is complicit in indulging these wasteland habits. In the space that remains, I will briefly plot three reservoirs within the church's own theological tradition. These reservoirs promise to recover the value of time and bodies to rewild the human wasteland by transforming it into a biblical wilderness wherein God addresses his people.

Resurrection

The first reservoir is the doctrine of the resurrection, which resituates humanity in (and with) time. It also reclaims the true value of the human body as secured by Christ's own resurrection. First, the doctrine of the resurrection reminds us that we live in the wake of the fullness of Christ's work in time. Our life is secured in Christ; we need not parcel up our time in frantic pursuit of the things of the world. Second, Christ's resurrection reminds us that time's purpose is complete. There is no "progress" to be

59. Brock, "Kierkegaard, Theology, and the Information Society," 469–70.

made; we are only to wait attentively for the apocalyptic revealing of the children of God for which all of creation eagerly awaits (Rom 8:19–23). Third, Christ's resurrection secures time from homogenous monotony, anchoring it between the fact of Christ's historical resurrection and the truth of his return at the resurrection of the dead. Christians know they reside "in the middle, [where] in the utterly inconceivable critical point between the before and after lies a creation, more strictly speaking: a new creation."[60] In anticipation of the resurrection of the dead, all saints of the church stand together as true "contemporaries"; they serve the God of the living, not the dead. Disciples can walk free of the illusion that any coordinated "simultaneity" between people can truly unite them in dialogue. They are free to address one another, and the world (1 Cor 15:12–15), because the simultaneous truth and reality of the resurrection grounds their speech. They are exhorted, "Sleeper, awake! Rise from the dead" (Eph 5:14) and they are freed by Christ to do so, because of his resurrection.

The doctrine of resurrection also rescues the body from commodification. First, the resurrection grounds the truth of Christian speech in a hope in which the individual Christian's own body has a stake. Barth observes how in 1 Corinthians 15, Paul responds to those who question the reality of resurrection by "[jerking] the questioner and spectator out of [their] comfortable position and [setting them] right in the midst of the struggle, in which the resurrection is truth."[61] As a result, we must not simply believe some vague fairy tale truth about heaven. Instead, we acknowledge and claim that it is this body of ours which will one day experience resurrection. This claim puts us back onto the playing field as witnesses of the truth and away from the sidelines where our speech is decoupled from our bodies. In this regard, the Christian martyr is the one who ultimately repairs bodies and truth. Energized by the reality of Christ's resurrection and the hope of their own, they stake their body on the claim that Christ is the risen and reigning Lord.[62] There is a perfect union between their claim that Christ is Lord and their willingness to back up this claim with their life.[63] At the

60. Barth, *Resurrection of the Dead*, loc. 2549.

61. Barth, *Resurrection of the Dead*, loc. 2738.

62. Radner, *Profound Ignorance*, 167, 220–21.

63. Reclaiming Martyrs' Day as a celebration of the church and opportunity to lift up stories of martyrs as examples (not idols) of this union between speech and life would be another appropriate practice to resist the decoupling of bodies and speech. (I am grateful to Rev. Lydia Lockhart for drawing attention to this historic church celebration in conversation.)

same time that they fully unite their speech and body, the martyr—as does every Christian disciple—acknowledges that their body is not their own. It is claimed by the name of Christ. Christians who know the truth of the resurrection of the dead receive and conceive of their earthly mortal bodies as a gift to be handed over to the same Lord who handed over his body to be broken for the sake of his church.

Sabbath

The second reservoir is Sabbath. Sabbath reclaims time from its fragmented, anchorless, suspended homogenization in the human wasteland for what it truly is: the arena of encounter. Unlike temples or buildings or online forums, Sabbath is the true architecture where humans encounter and engage one another, and God.[64] It is an architecture of time rather than space. Yet technical civilization, Abraham Heschel observes, insists on expending time to gain space.[65] (Hence how media apps spatialize communication on the surfaces of so many scrolling screens.) This spatialization of time puts us into the world of things.[66] We forget that the "higher goal of spiritual living is not to amass a wealth of information, but to face sacred moments."[67] Sabbath cultivates those moments in which God and humanity put down their labors and speak with one another as they rest together in God. But Sabbath does more than create an oasis of dialogue within time that reinfuses and reorients the rest of the week. Sabbath reminds of the coming eschaton; it is a foretaste of the true Sabbath rest which awaits humanity at the end of time. In this way, Sabbath practice reminds those receiving it where they are situated in time.[68] The church would do well to reclaim a practice of Sabbath, not in a spirit of legalism, but in a Spirit of articulate and creative hope—a Spirit that replenishes the dry ground of wasteland existence.[69]

64. Heschel, *Sabbath*, 8.

65. Heschel, *Sabbath*, 13.

66. Heschel, *Sabbath*,14.

67. Heschel, *Sabbath*, 15.

68. Heschel, *Sabbath*, 10.

69. For an excellent work on Barth's Sabbath theology which resists such legalism, see Lilley, "At the Invitation of the God Who Rests."

Eucharist

If Sabbath reclaims time from the wasteland, the Eucharist reclaims bodies. As in any shared meal, those partaking become composed and sustained by the same nutrients, the same earth. The sharing of food itself facilitates an exchange and discourse that serves to bond and unite different bodies.[70] What is more, in the Eucharist the body itself is wrested from its commodification by the human wasteland to serve a genuine symbolic exchange. Christ's body—the *Word*—given over to us, nurtures our body with meaning and incorporates us into dialogue with God and our fellow creatures. Stated differently, the bread and the wine offer us a transcendent, nourishing, and celebratory feast within the exhausting and dreary immanence of our human-made wasteland.

Conclusion

For all of this, perhaps the real reason we cannot address one another in the current technocratic wasteland is because we lack passion. True passion is willing to suffer in one's body over time. Maybe it is not just because our mediums of communication diminish time and bodies, training us in shallow habits of discourse, that we have nothing to say. Perhaps we have nothing to say because we are incapable of passion, resigned to barter our bodies and punctuated "likes" in the circulation of goods on the grand market of our wasteland existence. Indeed, as Baudrillard suggests, "ecstasy"—the collapse of difference and hypertrophy of communicative exchange—"is the opposite of passion."[71] In our commodification of time and bodies we have relinquished our willingness to suffer, and thus our ability to speak and listen.

But the Christ follower knows that Christ's passion and resurrection has inaugurated the time of our passion and resurrection, the time in which we can—in some inscrutable way with Paul—fill up in our flesh what is still lacking in regard to Christ's affliction for the sake of his body, the church (Col 1:24). In our rhythmic resting together and feasting together we also

70. For this reason, I think churches would do well to reclaim the context of the Eucharist from its reductionistic "dot and thimble" forms of crackers and grape juice from its Passover context as a shared meal. Streett, *Subversive Meals*, accounts how this early Christian practice adopted, yet subverted, the practice of the Greco-Roman patron sponsored meal, exchanging its hierarchized values with egalitarian Christ-based ones.

71. Baudrillard, *Ecstasy of Communication*, 29.

prepare to suffer together, even as we eagerly await our final Sabbath rest, our wedding feast, our resurrection. Indeed,

> We can live this life only to the degree that we know that the reconciliation is already won, and that in Jesus Christ word and sight, proclamation and experience, space and time, are united. . . . Based on this certainty, without which we have nothing to live for and without which the conflict would be intolerable, we can return to the daily struggle to make the word resound, alone and unshackled. During the space of time that separates us from this final sight, may the word resound for human freedom and for God's truth.[72]

Until that day, the church may continue to take up her post as a voice crying in the wilderness, addressing any who would hear: prepare the way of the Lord.

Bibliography

Anderson, Bernhard W. *Understanding the Old Testament*. 3rd ed. Englewood Cliffs, NJ: Prentice-Hall, 1975.

Barth, Karl. *The Resurrection of the Dead*. Eugene, OR: Wipf & Stock, 2003. Kindle.

Baudrillard, Jean. *The Ecstasy of Communication*. Los Angeles: Semiotext(e), 2012.

Bauman, Zygmunt. *Liquid Modernity*. Cambridge: Polity, 2000.

Benjamin, Ruha. *Race after Technology: Abolitionist Tools for the New Jim Code*. Medford, MA: Polity, 2019.

Bringhurst, Robert. *The Elements of Typographic Style*. 2nd ed. Point Roberts, WA: Hartley & Marks, 1996.

Brock, Brian. "Kierkegaard, Theology, and the Information Society." In *T&T Clark Companion to the Theology of Kierkegaard*, edited by Aaron Edwards and David Gouwens, 453–72. London: Bloomsbury, 2019.

Buber, Martin. *I and Thou*. Translated by Walter Arnold Kaufmann. New York: Simon & Schuster, 1970.

"Church Service Goes Into Record 7th Overtime." *Babylon Bee*, November 26, 2018. https://babylonbee.com/news/church-service-goes-into-record-7th-overtime.

Eliade, Mircea, and Willard R. Trask. *The Sacred and the Profane: The Nature of Religion*. San Diego: Harcourt, 1987.

Eliot, T. S. "The Waste Land." https://www.poetryfoundation.org/poems/47311/the-waste-land.

Ellul, Jacques. *The Humiliation of the Word*. Minneapolis: Eerdmans, 1985.

———. *The New Demons*. Translated by C. Edward Hopkin. New York: Seabury, 1975.

———. *The Technological Society: A Penetrating Analysis of Our Technical Civilization and of the Effect of an Increasingly Standardized Culture on the Future of Man*. Translated by John Wilkinson. New York: Vintage, 2011.

Fukuyama, Francis. *The End of History and the Last Man*. New York: Free, 2006.

72. Ellul, *Humiliation of the Word*, 269.

Hallowell, John. Review of *The New Demons*, by Jacques Ellul. *Journal of Church and State* 21 (1979) 333–35.

Heschel, Abraham Joshua. *The Sabbath: Its Meaning for Modern Man*. New York: Farrar, Straus, & Giroux, 2005.

Jennings, Willie James. *The Christian Imagination: Theology and the Origins of Race*. New Haven: Yale University Press, 2010. Kindle.

Jiang, Manyu. "The Reason Zoom Calls Drain Your Energy." *BBC*, April 22, 2020. https://www.bbc.com/worklife/article/20200421-why-zoom-video-chats-are-so-exhausting.

Johannes, Fabian. *Time and the Other: How Anthropology Makes Its Object*. New York: Columbia University Press, 1983.

John Paul II. *Man and Woman He Created Them: A Theology of the Body*. Edited by Michael Waldstein. Boston: Pauline Books & Media, 2006.

Lilley, David. "At the Invitation of the God Who Rests: The Fidelity-Producing Sabbath Ethic of Karl Barth's Doctrine of Creation." PhD diss., University of Aberdeen, 2018.

Picard, Andrew, and Jaimee van Gemerden. "A Theological Engagement with T. S. Eliot's Waste Land in the Context of COVID-19." *Crucible*, October 12, 2020. https://crucible.hymnsam.co.uk/articles/2020/october/articles/a-theological-engagement-with-t-s-eliot-s-the-waste-land/.

Radner, Ephraim. *A Profound Ignorance: Modern Pneumatology and Its Anti-Modern Redemption*. Waco, TX: Baylor University Press, 2019.

———. *A Time to Keep: Theology, Mortality, and the Shape of a Human Life*. Waco, TX: Baylor University Press, 2016.

Rollison, Jacob Marques. *A New Reading of Jacques Ellul: Presence in the Postmodern World*. Lanham, MD: Lexington, 2020.

Sechrest, Love L., et al., eds. *Can "White" People Be Saved? Triangulating Race, Theology, and Mission*. Missiological Engagements. Downers Grove, IL: IVP Academic, 2018.

Streett, R. Alan. *Subversive Meals: An Analysis of the Lord's Supper under Roman Domination during the First Century*. Eugene, OR: Pickwick, 2013.

Swinton, John. *Becoming Friends of Time: Disability, Timefullness, and Gentle Discipleship*. Waco, TX: Baylor University Press, 2018.

United Nations Convention to Combat Desertification. "The United Nations Decade for Deserts (2010–2020) and the Fight against Desertification." *UNCCD*, August 10, 2020. https://www2.unccd.int/actions/united-nations-decade-deserts-2010-2020-and-fight-against-desertification#:~:text=fight%20against%20Desertification-,The%20United%20Nations%20Decade%20for%20Deserts%20(2010%2D2020)%20and,that%20is%20slowly%20being%20degraded..

Wagenfuhr, Greg. *Plundering Eden*. Eugene, OR: Cascade, 2020.

Walters, James. *Baudrillard and Theology*. New York: T&T Clark, 2012.

Chapter Three

The Desert

Recapitulating and Going Beyond Ellul

Gregory Wagenfuhr

In many ways this rediscovered essay on "The Desert" offers Ellul's theological perspective and method in a nutshell: prioritizing the revelation of God in history and thus in narrative and relationship. Long before narrative theology was a widely known approach, Ellul recognized theology must not be done in ontological categories, nor in moral prescriptions, nor even through the lens of personal experience. Rather, Ellul believed theology is the revelation of God *in history of history*; the inbreaking of a divine narrative into the false and absurd narratives of human construction (myth).[1]

As such, theology is movement. It is a dialogue, a relationship, not an image or icon. But this movement has a design, an architecture, as Ellul's book *Apocalypse* explores in the book of Revelation.[2] Theology occupies the meeting point of time and eternity in space in the person of Jesus Christ. It is the radical inbreaking of the Wholly Other.[3] This inbreaking dislocates humans. It questions their stories, their justifications, their own creations. It liberates through exile in the wilderness. Indeed, the presence of God leads to the necessary judgment of the world as the Platonic world of imitative

1. My PhD thesis, "Revelation and the Sacred Reconsidered," covers this Ellulian movement in greater detail.

2. See Rollison, *Presence in the Postmodern World*, for full coverage of this movement and architecture.

3. The influence of the early Karl Barth should be evident here.

shadows that it is. Only, it reveals that humans are not chained prisoners in a cave, but puppet masters, constructing a world of simulacra and calling it reality. This is the human desert, of which Ellul speaks in this essay.[4] This desert is the place where humans are incapable of encountering God, but it is also the place where God appears to liberate the self-alienated captives and lead them to reconciliation.

As revelation in history of history, the divine narrative of meaning does not end with the close of Scripture, even though this is where the authoritative commentary on history ends. For Ellul, the Bible comments on all of history, not simply the historical events it narrates. It is by engaging with this authoritative commentary that one can re-narrate the narratives of one's own milieu in relationship with God.

And yet, Ellul has a striking thesis, that God has abandoned us and is silent in the modern world. According to Ellul, the modern world is particularly devoid of meaning because it has begun to occupy a wholly self-enclosed technical milieu of its own creation. The mythological systems of modernity are so effective that they have driven the voice of God out of hearing. One gets the sense from Ellul that he thinks God will not bother speaking where God knows he is not going to be heard. Thus, Ellul's theological reinterpretation of the modern milieu quite nearly aligns with Israel's captivity in Egypt.

By this dual reading of the Word of God and the situation of humanity today, Ellul elicits what God might say were he to speak. This is what we will briefly survey in this Chapter, with the caveat that this synchronic summary of Ellulian thought overlooks changes in Ellul's work over time.[5] It is with the dead and silent Ellulian *corpus*, not unlike with the living but ostensibly silent God, that we must freely and responsibly interpret.

4. As Ellul puts it in *The Humiliation of the Word*, 189–90: "But was I also supposed to take the freed prisoner by the hand, make him my pupil, and teach him what he should and could do? Doesn't this purely negative deed produce freedom? Now that he is unfettered, the person can stand up, begin to walk, and choose where he wants to go; he could do none of this before. Well, let him do it! But only he can do it, and if he prefers to stay hunched up in his prison wishing for his chains back, what further positive deed can I do for him?"

5. Rollison traces the synchronic changes to Ellul's thought in *Presence in the Postmodern World*.

The Word and Meaning

Before speaking of creation it is vital to understand that one of Ellul's major theological assumptions is that interpretation is necessary for meaning. Ellul believes interpretation is not something to which we turn when there is misunderstanding, because for him, all experience is always-already interpreted.[6] In the absence of the word of God, meaning is thus constructed with the resources available to human creatures, and therefore meaning necessarily is false as it leaves out who is absent: the Creator of the heavens, the earth, and everything in both.

Creation

For Ellul, creation does not establish ontological norms that must be rediscovered to attain true moral uprightness before the Creator-Judge. Rather, the period of creation is itself completed and God ceases to act. For Ellul, the major point of creation is the Word of God. In "The Desert," he ignores New Testament passages about creation (e.g. John 1; Heb 11:3) and prioritizes the Genesis account, thereby questioning *creatio ex nihilo* to highlight God as speaking into the wilderness, which in the Ancient Near East was a symbol of chaos. While Ellul is inaccurate on a few points here,[7] his main point holds. God is the one who speaks order, who creates by the very act of interpretation or judgment, and God does this in the context of what would seem the ultimate desert of chaos.[8]

The creation of humans as the image of God is the creation of a species capable of speaking, hearing, and interpreting.[9] As such, humans are

6. There are some significant thematic overlaps between Ellul and Martin Heidegger and the phenomenological school. Ellul, however, refused to engage Heidegger because of his Nazism. Ellul, *Living Faith*, 79; Ellul, *Ethics of Freedom*, 295; Ellul, *Reason for Being*, 148. See also Rognon, *Jacques Ellul*, 305–7, 323–25. But Ellul saw that their humanism was itself a vain attempt at creating a new meaning and new history based on humanity alone. It was vain because the fruit of this tree was that major thinkers like Heidegger and Sartre were caught up in the "collective imbecility" of the mass movements of Nazism and Stalinsim respectively. Ellul, *What I Believe*, 63.

7. Namely, *barah* is a uniquely divine action in the OT, and so it is not unfair to attempt to give it a uniquely divine rendering beyond "fabrication." See Wagenfuhr, *Plundering Eden*, 152–53, for more on this subject.

8. However, I argue that chaos is a human state of mind or experience rather than a kind of real reality. Wagenfuhr, *Plundering Eden*, 28–31.

9. Ellul writes in *Humiliation of The Word*, 45: "God speaks. We must answer him.

uniquely capable of engaging in the relationship of love that characterizes God. Such love requires that humans be autonomous and free. This freedom enables humans to lie, to intentionally misinterpret and falsely narrate. Such freedom allows for the possibility of breaking the relationships of love and truth displayed by the Creator for his creation.[10]

Freedom and the Seventh Day

Ellul believed that God's rest on the seventh day of creation is the enduring state of the whole history of the world. God ceased to act as the Creator because the creation was complete. His rest is not silence, but the rest of satisfaction in an enduring relationship of love with his creation. But God is not the Aristotelean Prime Mover, or first cause. This would imply a relationship of necessity that binds God to always be acting as Creator for the creation to continue its existence.[11] Creation is free, and this means free-from God as the omni-causal power whose providence foreordained everything that comes to pass. History is not the cause of events, it is the interpretation of them. The word of God is active and capable of transforming the direction of events, but it is not providence, a belief Ellul thinks is a subversion of Christianity that came through Islamic influence.[12] So, God's rest is the freedom of creation to act, and God's interventions in creation are always liberative (through judgment).

Although it is tempting to see Ellul as arguing for Open Theism, or even a modified type of Deism, Ellul does not fit within either of these theological categories. Against Deism, Ellul's God speaks and intervenes even

God creates human beings as speaking beings. Perhaps this is one of the meanings of the image of God: one who responds and is responsible; a counterpart who will dialogue, who is both at a certain distance and has the ability to communicate. The human being is the only one, out of the entire creation, who is capable of language. Like God who speaks or God who is said to speak, humanity has this capacity which comes from its creator. Speech constitutes human specificity, just as it constitutes the specificity of God as compared with all other gods. God summons a person through the word, and induces him to speak in dialogue. If God is freedom, there is someone there to live out freedom. If God is love, there is someone to respond to love through the word. The human word exists only because it is a product of the Word of God: I would not speak if you had not previously called me. 'Even before a word is on my tongue, O Lord, thou knowest it altogether,' (Ps. 139:4)."

10. Ellul, *What I Believe*, 23.

11. Ellul, *What I Believe*, 152–66.

12. Ellul, *Subversion of Christianity*, 107.

though he created a creation capable of autonomous continuity. Against Open Theism, Ellul's God speaks an authoritative interpretative word, predestines creation to a divinely chosen end, while participating in history. Where Deism and Open Theism are more or less ontological statements about God, each fruit of different Enlightenment philosophies (e.g., empiricism and Hegelianism), Ellul comes to understand the character of God through the revelation in the Bible as the one whose love is characterized by interventions for liberation, to reestablish the freedom of the rest of his Seventh Day. For Ellul, the type of religious metaphysics involved in both Deism and Open Theism are attempts at binding God and destroying love by creating a predictive divine order. Ellul's God descends in a disorienting revelation that liberates people to responsibility in freedom.[13]

Temptation, Alienation, and Abandonment

In freedom, humans fall into their own alienations. The three temptations of Jesus are quite often used by Ellul as the divine word on all human temptation.[14] Jesus was tempted in every way we are (Heb 4:15). These economic, political, and spiritual temptations that Jesus resisted are what humans fall prey to, and in so doing, break their relationship with God and need Jesus to restore that relationship. This leads humans into a kind of wilderness or desert, a world of silence in which God's voice has been muted by rebellion. The silencing of God is the descent into unmeaning, and it demands the construction of meaning. Constructing meaning is not simply done in word, but in concrete and in spiritual power. For, the order of alienation creates its own evil powers, its own evil logic. Powers are created beyond human control, but not separated from human existence. These powers are what actively enslave and oppress people.

It is when these powers are empowered, served, and worshipped that humans are alienated beyond any hope of self-rescue. While Ellul believes in human freedom, he is not a Pelagian or even semi-Pelagian. God alone can break through the authority of the principalities and powers with his

13. See Ellul's lengthy discussion on Revelation and religion in chapter 16 of *Living Faith*.

14. For example, Ellul, *Si tu es le fils de Dieu*, 70–85; Ellul, *Défi et le nouveau*, 984–86; Ellul, *Anarchy and Christianity*, 57–59; Ellul, *Ethics of Freedom*, 52–62; Ellul, *Living Faith*, 139–40; Ellul, *Meaning of the City*, 114; Ellul, *Reason for Being*, 298.

Word and so liberate a people who are incapable of liberating themselves, try as they might.

The concrete form of human alienation is in the very works of humanity, its cultures, its architecture, its cities, and civilization. All of these are the concretization of human rebellion and refusal to live in the desert of their own making by their rupture with God as Ellul describes at length in *Meaning of the City*. In the city, powers beyond human means are created. In the city, humans totally abandon God because they have the means of doing so. Satan's words are spoken in the city, and the Word of God appears in the desert. It is by listening to our own babblings in our own isolated and self-enclosed milieux, a constructed mirror of ourselves, that God is silenced. The voice of God can be drowned in a ceaseless transmission of sound, image, propaganda, and political illusion. Modern life so perfects alienation that humans are now more than ever subjected to a predestination and providence of the Evil One.[15] We live within a closed-off world that has structurally silenced God, as Ellul argues in *Hope in Time of Abandonment*. So, God has left off speaking and abandoned us to our self-made desert.[16]

Election and Revelation

And yet, God will not remain silent forever, nor forsake his people forever. God chooses a people within the human wastelands of their making; people like Abraham, or Israel under Moses. God's choice of a people is, at least later in his life, universal. Because, while only some are liberated in time, in eternity, all will be freed from the reign of sin and alienation. This is what love demands, Ellul says.

But liberation must act from the outside, and this only can come by revelation. It is the Word of God speaking into the human desert of so-called civilization that liberates people. This Word became flesh in Jesus Christ who is, for Ellul following Barth, elect humanity in himself. The ultimate remnant of the elect people of God in Jesus represents the whole.[17] The word of God is the breaking-in of God into the human world, and this creates a breakdown of the human world that enables the act of liberation.

15. In the first chapter of *Ethics of Freedom*, Ellul argues that the best modern term for the biblical understanding of sin is "alienation."

16. See Ellul, *What I Believe*, ch. 14.

17. Ellul, *What I Believe*, 39.

The revelation of God is a critique of human civilization which opens the ears of the elect to hear an alternative word and so be freed.

Liberation

Thus, God liberates his people by demythologizing the world, by desacralizing its sacred values and systems.[18] Liberation is the judgment of the powers by holding them up to shame (Col 2:15). But by disarming the power of what has been held to be sacred, God destroys the very fabric of the false-history humans have created. This leads people into the wilderness or desert, the only location where the Word of God may be heard. The Word of God is a renewal of relationship, and this can only come after the structures of alienation are destroyed by being named what they are: a desert or wasteland. Such a liberation is incredibly challenging and few desire it. For it is a desire for a non-world, chaos, and meaninglessness, that must precede the hearing of a new word and a new interpretation of history. God brings chaos to the human false-cosmos which is, in reality, the only true chaos.[19] True history only begins after the false history has come to an end, and the liminal space where false history might come to an end is the desert. But the desert is not a place to which one can retreat to leave history. The desert is not a place to escape the world in solitude. It is a place to meet God. In this way, Ellul avoids and critiques Platonic, Hindu, and Buddhist understandings of spirituality seeking deconstruction of the self to gain unity with the One. For Ellul, liberation is only the end of the false history, it is not itself the goal. Liberation is the end that begins, the void into which God speaks into the old and creates something new. As spoken prophetically in Isaiah 43:19:

> I am about to do a new thing;
> now it springs forth; do you not perceive it?
> I will make a way in the wilderness
> and rivers in the desert.

It is in God's desert that God re-forms a people, gives them a new identity by declaring them to be separate or holy. Only after liberation can sin be

18. Ellul, *New Demons*, 209–28.

19. See my *Plundering Eden* for a fuller discussion of this subject.

perceived as sin.[20] By naming a people God begins their history anew in relationship with him, and thus in concert with them.

Reconciliation and Presence

By tracing the theme of the desert in the essay of that title, Ellul leaves off some key biblical themes he covers elsewhere. The desert is not the place where reconciliation comes to its fullness, as in the Promised Land. Nor is the desert the sign of the fulfilment and presence of the kingdom. The desert, rather, is a station; a transitory location; a place passed over as one is on-the-way to the Promised Land, fulfillment, and the kingdom. After leaving Egypt, and leaving the desert, the people of God under Joshua, and those under the reign of Jesus, enter into the promise of God for life ordered by his narration. This taking of leave in the desert is God's invitation into history and meaning.

But Ellul dwells on the desert intentionally here and throughout much of his work because that is his understanding of our location now. In response to the death of God theologians and secularization narratives in sociology that were popular in his time (and still are to some extent), Ellul believes that the Word of God can disappear from our midst. The presence of the kingdom of God is not always and necessarily progressively increasing in its revelation. Rather, it can for a time be effaced by subjection of the church to the world and the abandonment of the Spirit from within.

But there is hope. "We are not marching toward the Kingdom of God," Ellul writes, though "the Kingdom of God is bursting violently into our times, into our milieu.[21] Ellul views God as breaking into our time, here and now, with his kingdom, which requires judgment and the critique of the world as it perceives itself. This is a liberation for the sake of reconciliation, and it is the very presence of the eschaton here and now. But the bursting of God into human history is not a stark and bare self-revelation that strips individual people of will and freedom by overwhelming them with naked presence. This would be the death of humanity! Ellul believes, "There is no theophany of the God of the Bible, because he is the one who defers to a greater reality in the future."[22] Rather, God is revealed in the Word through the man Jesus, who is only ever seen as a man. Because God comes

20. Ellul, *Perspectives on Our Age*, 85.

21. Ellul, *Hope in Time of Abandonment*, 172.

22. Ellul, *Hope in Time of Abandonment*, 173.

as a humble man who speaks in a particular context, God is calling for a renewed conversation, a renewed relationship.

The Christian in the World Now

The presence of the kingdom of God comes in a form that is perceptible and otherworldly, but not with power.[23] This presence gives rise to actions based on the interpretative Word of God that seeks to make God's history apparent. It is "revolutionary" because the presence of the kingdom re-narrates history in other terms.[24] For Ellul, what matters is not some kind of bare, objective fact of reality. Such phenomena do not exist uninterpreted. What matters is how these facts are narrated, whether in the false myths of human construction or the divine revelation of history. It is the Word of God that upholds the world amid human freedom aimed at self-destruction. Indeed, the very fact of human freedom permits human history to be falsely constructed. It is in the silence of God that human history lives and moves and has its false-being. So, the Word of God has to be made alive through the Spirit.

Eschatology: Recapitulation and Judgment

Ellul's eschatology later in life turned toward universal salvation and recapitulation, a view derived from Irenaeus of Lyon.[25] For Ellul, the end of history must be seen as the summing of all things up by God in Jesus, and so the bringing of all things once again into the Seventh Day and the presence of God. This does not eliminate judgment but reframes judgment in a way that applies only to the works of humans rather than their being. God re-narrates all of history in himself, and this judges human history, destroying evil works, though refining his people through the fire.

Going Beyond Ellul's Desert

Ellul's strengths are also representative of his weaknesses, and "The Desert" shows the latter well. Ellul's great strength lies in his critical ability, and he

23. Ellul, *Apocalypse*, 79.

24. Ellul, *Presence in the Modern World*, 31.

25. Ellul, *What I Believe*, ch. 16.

shows this by analyzing biblical themes and comparing these with the present situation and reading ourselves into the narrative movement. He does this here with the desert or wilderness, but elsewhere with the city, money, hope, freedom, and more. He is also uniquely skilled and provocative in his commentaries on specific books: Jonah, Ecclesiastes, Revelation, and Kings.[26] But he does not offer his own eschatological recapitulation of these diverse themes and texts. That is, he does not offer much in the way of a constructive theology that helps give direction to the people of God in the desert. Absent from "The Desert" is any consideration of the opposite of the biblical perspective of the desert, which might be hoped for and expected to help define the desert by means of its contrast in the garden of Eden, Promised Land, and kingdom of God. For it is within these biblical locations that the desert must fit in order to make sense of God's action and history's meaning. By combining ecclesiology, eschatology, and ecology, we will see that Ellul's narrative movement and perspective on God as the author of history generates a more robust biblical perspective.

Ecclesiology

Perhaps Ellul's greatest theological weakness is his ecclesiology. There are many possible reasons for this—the influence of Kierkegaard, his disillusion with the mediocrity of the institution in his day, his belief that the Spirit was absent from the churches of his time, and his important focus on the individual to the neglect of a mature image of the church as a community. Ellul was not simply a radical individualist, as might be assumed from his writings. He was interested in liberation, and one of the greatest sources of alienation in his and our own time is group-identity, particularly in the nation/state and sexuality.[27] Rather than simply being a division between group and individual, Ellul understood that modern group-identities were radically different to those of old. Modern groups are part of "mass society" in which a person is alone in the crowd, but acting in concert with the crowd.[28] This massification of society alienates the individual because her life is determined by structures and techniques rather than by individual

26. *Judgement of Jonah*, *Reason for Being*, *Apocalypse*, and *The Politics of God and the Politics of Man* respectively.

27. Ellul, *New Demons*, 70–87.

28. Ellul and Troude-Chastenet, *Jacques Ellul*, 83.

will or organic community.[29] So Ellul describes the freedom of mass society: "On vacation we freely choose our route, though at the same moment that millions of others are making similar free choices."[30] Mass society is no real society at all, it is the absence of culture, since technique is itself the absence of culture.[31] It is the formation of a monolithic, predictable, and controllable bunching of individuals whose possibility of meaning is lost in this technical slavery. Liberation for Ellul is not anti-communal. He holds out the possibility of intentionally joining a people who love one another in freedom. This is a kind of elitism inherent in a voluntary organization within a mass society.[32] But Ellul does not describe what this might look like as the people of God.

Ellul's emphasis on ethics and command reveals that he believes the Christian life is one of individual action rather than community-belonging. For, ethics is an inherently individualistic enterprise that comes by breakdowns of organic communities and social roles therein, hence its rise in the so-called Axial Age with urbanization and breakdown of organic tribal communities.[33] Taboo transforms into ethics by means of alienation. Ironically, it is the very early massification of humanity in the *polis* and imperial cities that gives rise to the possibility of the church as a body that transcends natural categories of unity, and yet, it is this body that is itself critical of the very power structures and exploitation that enable such a *polis* to exist.[34] So, within the notion of the church lies the very force of liberation that Ellul seeks for the individual through ethics. Individual ethics, however, are unmaintainable without mutual support—unless one retreats to the theological desert he critiques in "The Desert." It is only by the creation of alternative communities to which one is able to be *liberated to*, that one is able to live in freedom.

29. Ellul, *Technological Society*, 206–8.

30. Ellul, *Technological Bluff*, 373.

31. See Ellul *Technological Bluff*, ch. 6.

32. Ellul and Troude-Chastenet, *Jacques Ellul*, 83; See also Ellul, *Propaganda*, 90–99; Ellul, *Technological Society*, 332–35.

33. The recently published and translated Ellul, *To Will and To Do*, does formulate what Ellul calls a "communal ethic" (cf. 38–46), but Ellul generally does focus more on the individual in his work.

34. It is to be remembered that the population of Classical Athens was two-thirds slave. Scott, *Against the Grain*, 156.

I have elsewhere offered an ecclesiology deeply inspired by Ellul,[35] so let me summarize some basic points here. The Bible is a story of two peoples from the third chapter unto the last—those who are being reconciled to God, and those to whom this people are sent as ambassadors of God, bearers of his Word. These two peoples persist. The final pages of Revelation do not conclude with a final unity, but with a continuation of this situation. Thus, we might summarize the Bible's narrative most simply as God becoming king of the world according to his character, with and through his people (*and not humanity as a whole*) participating in this conquest through divine love, and through this process his people becoming the image of God in Christ. I hesitate to use the word *love* here to describe how this process unfolds, as Ellul makes it essential to the image of God, which then means that he uses human examples of love as a heuristic to understand the character of God in a breakdown of his usual logic of trusting first to the Word of God for revelation.[36] This is most evident in his later conviction of universal salvation in which his logic begins with the statement, "God is love," but he does not examine this character trait as revealed in the movement of the biblical narrative.[37]

Thus, all that Ellul draws out in his theological works is to be incorporated into the life of the body of Christ. The Christian finds maturity in the body of Christ, and it is in this context alone that true freedom is possible. It is only by union with Christ through his body that we can come to know love. Where Ellul spends much of his time considering what the desert of liberation looks like, he does not describe much the Promised Land to which we are heading as a people formed in exile. Indeed, it is in the desert that the people of God begin to be re-formed. To be people worthy of inheriting the kingdom of God, the people of God must become a people together. This involves speaking the Word of God to one another, loving one another as Christ loves us (even our enemy), working for one another's liberation from all forms of bondage to the world, and becoming a community in which the kingdom of God becomes plausible and tangible. From this point, the *ekklesia* can re-engage the world as ambassadors of Christ and his kingdom with confidence in their mutual support.

35. Wagenfuhr, *Plundering Eden*, 161–77.

36. To be sure, his reflections in *What I Believe*, ch. 7, "Lifelong Love," are inspiring and robust. But Ellul begins with human evolution and works towards the Christian life in union with Christ without mentioning that union with Christ is ecclesial.

37. Ellul, *What I Believe*, 189–93.

Eschatology

Ellul's eschatology of recapitulation has great promise. He acknowledges that the "end" is not out there in the future, but something invading the present, constituting a good understanding of Jewish apocalyptic thought. God's authoritative reinterpretation of human history will end with a form of universal salvation for all of creation. But, Ellul's universalism is highly dissonant with his deep emphasis on freedom and liberation. If God forcibly reconciles all things to himself in the end, it begs the question: why not now? Why does God change from this permissive freedom? Certainly, Ellul's thought shifted and his universalism was a later development, and it is not without promise. But the dissonances require a reworking of an Ellulian eschatology.

One of his chief interpretative errors, I would suggest, is in his understanding of the heavenly Jerusalem as a type of *aufhebung* (dialectical sublimation) of the garden of Eden. Ellul sees this, as many others have, as a movement from the garden to the city in which human history is appropriated into the eschaton.[38] In this way, human history is given meaning by some eternal presence before the face of God in concretized form. This is an anthropocentric eschatology that fails to acknowledge that the goods of human "progress" are, from the perspective of the rest of creation, evil and injurious. Reconciliation cannot occur where structures and symbols of oppression remain. The city itself is fruit of agrarian labor-surplus, built on the backs of the slaves of humans and of the creation itself.[39] Unless there be yokes, whips, and gibbets in the heavenly Jerusalem, neither can reconciliation be represented by a city itself. The cross does not reappear in the heavenly Jerusalem, though Jesus retains the marks of the slain lamb. The effects of history remain, but this does not require it to become a museum of human concrete achievements, which themselves are now obliterating the creation itself. That is, following Ellul here, the city itself is one of humanity's evil works that will be destroyed by the fire of God's judgment.

John of Revelation's use of the two cities of Babylon the Great and the heavenly Jerusalem follows from Ezekiel's use of forest imagery to represent two empires: Israel and Assyria. In Ezekiel 31 Israel is seen as the trees of the garden of Eden. Assyria, which itself was not known biblically for its forests, unlike Lebanon, was home to the famous hanging gardens, and

38. Ellul, *Meaning of the City*.

39. See Wagenfuhr, *Plundering Eden*; Scott, *Against the Grain*.

other palace architecture that simulated a microcosm of the world under the rule of the emperor. The contrast of Babylon with Jerusalem follows a similar logic, and a similar imaginative method. The City of God represents the reign of God in an extended throne room or palace which has expanded to cover all of creation, including Eden. The throne room is symbolized by the temple, and the city itself is an extension of the temple. The "house of God" is now among the whole of the earth, visible, and glorious. John then sees that all peoples come to do obeisance and pay tribute as an acknowledgment of the rightness of the king's rule.

Irenaeus of Lyon's idea of *anakephalaiosis*, or recapitulation, serves as the basis for Ellul's later eschatology, and is based in Ephesians 1:10.[40] But here again, Ellul misses the crucial context for Ephesians 1—the collective people of God, adopted as heirs with Christ of his kingdom. The uniting of all things in Christ, for Paul, is the eschatological victory of the people of God with Christ. Recapitulation cannot be discussed for *humanity* primarily, but must first be spoken of through the church as the body of Christ, which thus thrusts the church once again to the fore.

And so, we might modify Ellul's universal salvation, for the word *salvation* is incredibly misleading in Christian history, for it is not a fixed biblical category. Rather, it refers to liberation from evil and escape from the wrath of God in judgment.[41] The universal salvation in the Bible is liberation from the structures of sin at the final victory of Christ. But not all shall be saved from the wrath of God on the day of the Lord. The ultimate question then, is not whether people go to heaven or hell, which are not biblical categories here, but whether they are reconciled and join the kingdom of God and the people of God, or continue in rebellion, as signified in by the enduring presence of walls (and people outside of them) in Revelation 21–22. Ellul sees this judgment as merely the destruction of evil works, with individuals undergoing a separation between their being and their works so that they are saved, but nothing remains (as in 1 Cor 3:15). Here again Ellul misses the ecclesial nature of this judgment. This is not about concrete works judged on holiness, but whether a person has figuratively constructed their lives on the foundation of Jesus Christ and lived for the edification of the people of God, which is God's temple.

40. See Ellul, *What I Believe*, ch. 16.

41. See Wagenfuhr, *Unfortunate Words of the Bible*, 64–71.

Ecology

Although Ellul was an early figure in ecology, along with his friend Bernard Charbonneau, and an ecological activist, he devotes very little space to theological reflection on the non-human creation. His theology is thoroughly anthropocentric in ways consistent with historical Christian theology. For Ellul, all of creation is represented in Christ because Christ is the representation of humanity: "He signifies the salvation of all Israel and therefore of the human race and therefore of all creation."[42] Likewise, Ellul sees humanity as the mediator of creation to God,[43] a view shared with many Orthodox theologians, and one that Richard Bauckham discredits based on other biblical data.[44] Creation is able to praise God in its own language (e.g., Isa 55:12; Job 38:7). The stones can proclaim the good news of Jesus (Luke 19:40). Such a view leads to serious ecological problems that Ellul himself militates against. But beyond that, it also wrongly makes history anthropocentric in a way that does not fit biblical descriptions of God's relationship with other creatures who have existed before humans, as with Behemoth and Leviathan in Job, nor of the angels, whatever the reality of their being, nor even of the falling sparrows.

Because Ellul centers history around God's relationship with humanity, he unwittingly turns the pre-civilized or pre-human world into a historical desert, a land of unmeaning. The lesson of Job is clear, human counsel and human knowledge are painfully limited. There is meaning and history apart from human knowledge and apart from God's revelation to us. For God's relationship to his creation is meaningful according to its own kind, and it is good.

The incredible fruitfulness of humanity has prevented other creatures from fulfilling their creational mandate/blessing of being fruitful as well.[45] If Ellul is correct that history is given meaning by the revelation of God, we must suppose that there are other histories than the ones humans narrate. If God knows each hair on the heads of individual people and he knows each individual sparrow, he also has a direct and personal relationship with every creature of his creation, and the number of divine histories is therefore

42. Ellul, *What I Believe*, 39.

43. Ellul, *On Freedom, Love, and Power*, 34.

44. Bauckham, *Bible and Ecology*, 17.

45. See Wagenfuhr, *Plundering Eden*, 92.

nearly limitless. God has a story about that which we cannot and will never comprehend in far off galaxies.

An Eco-ecclesial-eschaton

Thus, ecclesiology is eschatology. Eschatology is ecological. And the three together round out a different perspective, but one still rooted in an Ellulian method. Uniting these critiques and ways forward, Ellul's theological method can be greatly strengthened by modifying his belief in *anakephalaiosis*. That God is summing up all things in Jesus is indeed the divine retelling of history, but it is not a forcible reconciliation by some divine propaganda. It is the inclusion of all diverse stories of each subatomic particle in the person of Jesus Christ as God becomes king over all creation. Within this, the people of God retain a particular place. Recapitulation is the mission of the church because it is the reconciling of all things in Christ. Recapitulation is fundamentally ecological in that it is aimed at the liberation of all creation from sin. And yet, is it not fitting that the desert might play a continued role in the new creation? After all, those symbols of chaos—the ocean and wilderness—are not enemies of God in his creation. They are incorporated too, and perhaps it is into a desert exile that God consigns those who will not be reconciled. This is the "outer darkness" of being outside of the camp. It is a place of weeping and gnashing of teeth, but could it not also be God's liberation of his enemies from the structures of their own alienation to experience the same freedom the people of God did in their own wilderness wanderings and exiles? The judgment of God that purges his creation from human counter-creations by fire will save sinners from the death that sin demands and leads to, and it will deposit these into the very place Cain, the patriarch of sin, himself refused to sojourn.

In conclusion, "The Desert" reveals key methods of Ellul's theology, just as it shows areas for improvement. We certainly live within the desert, a period in which God may seem to be silent, and with the human wasteland advancing at a logarithmic scale until we have come to the point of the collective suicide Ellul feared in *Presence in the Modern World*. Though, such a suicide will be wholly the unintentional consequences of the "collective imbecility"[46] of mass society.

I continue to perceive in Ellul after years of study a mentor who urges us on to continue his method, surpassing his conclusions and working to

46. Ellul, *What I Believe*, 63.

be the presence of the Word of God in an alienated world. But perhaps God has not abandoned us. Perhaps God is not silent. Perhaps it falls to the *ekklesia* to prophetically speak the word of God, lest the rocks themselves cry out in our stead.

Bibliography

Bauckham, Richard. *The Bible and Ecology*. Waco, TX: Baylor University Press, 2010.

Ellul, Jacques. *Anarchy and Christianity*. Translated by Geoffrey W. Bromiley. Eugene, OR: Wipf & Stock, 1991.

———. *Apocalypse*. Translated by Georgre W. Schreiner. New York: Seabury, 1975.

———. *Le défi et le nouveau*. Paris: La Table Ronde, 2007.

———. *The Ethics of Freedom*. Translated by Geoffrey W. Bromiley. London: Mowbrays, 1986.

———. *Hope in Time of Abandonment*. Translated by Geoffrey W. Bromiley. Grand Rapids: Eerdmans, 1973.

———. *The Humiliation of the Word*. Translated by Joyce Main Hanks. Grand Rapids: Eerdmans, 1985.

———. *The Judgment of Jonah*. Translated by Geoffrey W. Bromiley. Grand Rapids: Eerdmans, 1971.

———. *Living Faith*. Translated by Peter Heinegg. Eugene, OR: Wipf & Stock, 1983.

———. *Meaning of the City*. Translated by Denis Pardee. Eugene, OR: Wipf & Stock, 2011.

———. *New Demons*. Translated by C. Edward Hopkin. New York: Seabury, 1975.

———. *On Freedom, Love, and Power*. Translated by Willem Vanderburg. Toronto: University of Toronto Press, 2010.

———. *Perspectives on Our Age*. Edited by Willem Vanderburg. Toronto: House of Anansi, 2004.

———. *Presence in the Modern World*. Translated by Lisa Richmond. Eugene, OR: Cascade, 2016.

———. *Propaganda: The Formation of Men's Attitudes*. Translated by Konrad Kellen and Jean Lerner. New York: Vintage, 1975.

———. *Reason for Being*. Translated by Joyce Main Hanks. Grand Rapids: Eerdmans, 1989.

———. *Si tu es le fils de Dieu*. Worcester: Bayard, 1997.

———. *Subversion of Christianity*. Translated by Geoffrey W. Bromiley. Eugene, OR: Wipf & Stock, 2011.

———. *Technological Bluff*. Translated by Geoffrey W. Bromiley. Grand Rapids: Eerdmans, 1990.

———. *The Technological Society*. Translated by John Wilkinson. New York: Vintage, 1967.

———. *What I Believe*. Translated by Geoffrey W. Bromiley. Grand Rapids: Eerdmans, 1989.

———. *To Will and To Do: An Introduction to Christian Ethics, Volume II*. Translated by Jacob Marques Rollison. Eugene, OR: Cascade, 2021.

Ellul, Jacques, and Patrick Troude-Chastenet. *Jacques Ellul on Politics, Technology, and Christianity*. Eugene, OR: Wipf & Stock, 2011.

Rognon, Frédéric. *Jacques Ellul: Une pensée en dialogue*. Genève: Labor et Fides, 2009.

Rollison, Jacob Marques. *A New Reading of Jacques Ellul: Presence in the Postmodern World*. Lanham, MD: Lexington, 2020.

Scott, James C. *Against the Grain: A Deep History of Early States*. New Haven: Yale University Press, 2017.

Wagenfuhr, Gregory. *Unfortunate Words of the Bible*. Eugene, OR: Cascade, 2019.

———. *Plundering Eden: A Subversive Christian Theology of Creation and Ecology*. Eugene, OR: Cascade, 2020.

———. "Revelation and the Sacred Reconsidered: The Revelation of God in Christ as Desacralising 'Environmental Reorientation' in and beyond Jacques Ellul." PhD diss., University of Bristol, 2013.

Chapter Four

Watching and Managing in the Wasteland

EMILY BETH HILL

THE ARRIVAL OF THE COVID-19 virus in 2019, which spread around the globe through 2020, disrupted life as we knew it and plunged the world into confusion, sickness, and death. As lockdowns were enacted in North America and many people were unable to gather, churches were forced to ask fundamental questions about the nature of church itself. For example, how can we perform and receive the Eucharist online? Or, if we meet online and stream sermons, does that constitute *church*? As typical forms of Sunday gatherings and smaller community of faith meetings were stripped away, many churches entered a liminal space, a desert amidst the desolation of COVID-19.[1]

Liminal spaces are very difficult places to be, yet they are pregnant with the possibility of transformation. As Jacques Ellul writes, "The desert is *both good and bad: good* because it is the place to which God sends

1. We might consider other reasons the church in the West is in a desert: for example, the division amongst Christians within and across denominations, or the church's frequent idolatry, economic exploitation, and white supremacy, flowing from its captivity to Western culture. On such church division see Erickson, *Ephraim Radner, Hosean Wilderness, and the Church in the Post-Christendom West*. Regarding idolatry, exploitation, and white supremacy see Wright, *"Here Are Your Gods": Faithful Discipleship in Idolatrous Times*. Chapter 5 has an analysis of the rise and fall of nations in the Hebrew Bible with commentary on the situation in the Western World. See also Rah, *Prophetic Lament*.

[people] or [people encounter] God; but at the same time *bad* because it is a place of absence, deprivation, void, and chaos. Thus, it signifies *both* a promise and a threat."[2] In the desert, there can be disorientation, grief, and trauma wrought by loss of order, loss of control, loss of the way things used to be, and loss of typical ways of understanding and being. Yet, in the desert there can be clarity, hope, and healing when God meets human beings and reveals Godself and communicates God's Word clearly. As Ellul puts it, "The formlessness and the void is that which can give birth to form and which is waiting to be filled," and "the Word of God is that which alone which can give shape to and fill this absolute void."[3] But how do human beings cope with being in the desert when the clarity, hope, and healing do not materialize because God seems to be, or actually is, silent? Will churches wait patiently for the Word of God to stream into the wild and make a new way to a land of milk and honey, or will they cling to what they know to survive and make ends meet on their own terms? If the church is in the desert today, there are different ways it can respond to this "ambiguous place."[4] In this essay I want to examine the response of churches to life and death in the desert—this ambiguous place, our ambiguous place—in light of their uses of a particular technique that is unique to late-modernity stricken by the COVID-19 pandemic: surveillance capitalism.

Given Ellul's strong critiques of technology, it is fitting to investigate this pervasive and underexamined technique—especially as it pertains to the church's use of it. The theological and ethical questions surveillance capitalism raise depend on exactly how churches use it and what they imagine they are accomplishing. For our purposes, I want to ask what it means for churches to employ these technologies as they inhabit the desert, and more specifically, live in the light of God's own presence and knowledge in the desert. I will argue that any church's use of surveillance capitalism and its attendant techniques is equivalent to clinging to power and control in the desert, even if, as Ellul notes, the desert calls for "the abandonment of power in whatever form it appears."[5] Therefore, I want to use Ellul's work in and beyond this until now unpublished and untranslated essay to call the

2. Ellul, "The Desert," 10.
3. Ellul, "The Desert," 12.
4. Ellul, "The Desert," 10.
5. Ellul, "The Desert," 30.

church to non-power, and a different way of journeying in the desert: to remember the acts of God whose "steadfast love endures forever" (Ps 165).[6]

In the first section I introduce surveillance capitalism as a technique and outline its logic according to Shoshana Zuboff. In the second section I use Ellul's essay to reflect on churches' use of surveillance capitalism in the desert and draw in another desert encounter: God's self-revelation in Exodus 34. Finally, in the concluding section, I call the church to non-power and an alternative practice for waiting for God in the desert.

The Logic of Surveillance Capitalism

Churches are increasingly relying on the use of Google, Facebook, YouTube, and various mobile phone apps for ministry. An article in *The New York Times* revealed an array of partnerships that churches and religious organizations formed with Facebook, including a pastor seeking advice about "how to the build a church in a pandemic." The pastor, a leader at the Atlanta-based megachurch Hillsong said, "They are teaching us, we are teaching them."[7] Meanwhile, prominent Silicon Valley investors have lined up to bet on our prayer lives. *Christianity Today* reports that in 2021 venture capitalists invested $175 million into prayer apps—up from $100,000 in 2016.[8]

While some churches were forced to figure out online options during the pandemic, arguably COVID-19 has only accelerated existing trends. There has been a significant movement toward marketing-driven churches and other management inspired techniques as the decline in religious affiliation has increased in the West. For example, as early as 1988, George Barna wrote, "Based on careful study of data and the activities of American churches . . . the major problem plaguing the Church is its failure to embrace a marketing orientation in what has become a marketing-driven environment."[9] More broadly, in many cases the solution offered to church decline is a "'tool-kit' of practices related to *congregational uniqueness, entrepreneurial leadership,* and *management-inspired techniques.*"[10] Such

6. All Scripture references are NRSV unless otherwise noted, or as quoted in Ellul's manuscript.

7. Dias, "Facebook's Next Target."

8. Silliman, "Venture Capitalists See Profit in Prayer."

9. Barna, *Marketing the Church*, 23.

10. Shakespeare, *Being the Body of Christ*, 32.

proposals, in which the church is governed by efficiency imperatives and success is defined by the demands of productivity and optimization, are unsurprising considering Ellul's insight into the totalizing nature of technique. Ellul argues the extension of technique to every area of life "occurs all the more easily because technique is declared neutral." He continues, "In reality, when we say that technique seems neutral what we mean is that deep within ourselves we all think it is good. Technique is good because it extends the power of human beings, and means are justified today by the power that they give to human beings."[11] Despite many of the techniques at our disposal appearing to be inherently good because they are guarantors of efficiency and productivity, Ellul thinks such appearances are mirages in the "desert" of meaning and value.[12] Therefore, he urges, Christians must critically examine the age in which they live to see everything for what it really is and everyone for what they really are: under the Lordship of Christ. Christians must examine how any technology does or does not find its place in the kingdom ruled by this Lord, and through such examination discover an existence in which flawed means do not become ends in themselves and so distract from and compromise good ends.[13]

As churches have increased their uses of digital and mobile technologies in the wake of COVID-19, this examination is significant given these technologies intersect heavily with what Shoshana Zuboff has theorized as a new economic order: surveillance capitalism.[14] Zuboff describes surveillance capitalism as the systematic extraction of human behavior and personal experiences, developed into prediction products for sale to those who want to forecast, modify, and control human outcomes for their own ends and profit.[15]

Often the motivation for surveillance is thought about in terms of safety, though in the case of surveillance capitalism I would argue that churches do not necessarily know they are engaged in surveillance because the existence of it often is obscured. Consequently, the motivation is not always safety, and in some cases, it is vague if not totally unknown.

11. Ellul, *Presence in the Modern World*, 47.

12. Ellul, *Presence in the Modern World*, 49.

13. Ellul, *Presence in the Modern World*, 56–57.

14. A core part of Zuboff's argument is that surveillance capitalism was a human invention created at a point in time for a specific purpose: "It is not an inherent result of digital technology, nor is it a necessary expression of information capitalism." Zuboff, *Age of Surveillance Capitalism*, 85.

15. Zuboff, *Age of Surveillance Capitalism*, 8.

Nevertheless, Zuboff describes a process of "incursion, habituation, adaptation, and redirection"[16] in which technologies (mal)form people, groups, and entire societies to accept this rationality and its constituent practices so that the presence of this ubiquitous system of surveillance becomes a common sense and status quo. Sometimes people experience surveillance capitalism as something that cannot be escaped or avoided, in other instances people feel its manifestations as trivial annoyances, and in other cases still the tools and benefits it provides are seen as positive means to our own good ends. Given this, and a history of churches in North America being quite ready to adapt various technologies and media trends, it is unsurprising that churches utilize many platforms supported by surveillance capitalism without serious theological reflection.[17] For example, in the *New York Times* piece referenced earlier, one pastor said of Facebook, "Obviously there are different ways they . . . will serve their shareholders." But "from our vantage point, Facebook is a platform that allows us to build community, and connect with our community and accomplish our mission. So it serves I think everybody well."[18] This view exhibits a symptom of our technological society: to separate the means of communication embedded in a profit-maximizing, commercially-oriented, attention-grabbing enterprise from the church's identity as the body of Christ and her goals carried out in the Spirit.

In this section, I outline the logic of surveillance capitalism according to Zuboff, including its common commodity, products, and marketplace. In the next section I draw out further elements of the surveillance capitalist system as I consider the implications and ask questions of churches' uses of such technologies in the desert.

The Commodity

First, the commodity in surveillance capitalism is the personal life and experiences of human beings. Just as Karl Polanyi described how life, land, and economic exchange became subordinated to the market and became commodity fictions, Zuboff argues that surveillance capitalists have created

16. Zuboff, *Age of Surveillance Capitalism*, 139.

17. Dias, "Facebook's Next Target." For a history of the church's use of media and an argument to continue this adaptation see Horsfield, *From Jesus to the Internet*.

18. Dias, "Facebook's Next Target."

a new, zero cost commodity as the market has continued to innovate.[19] The new commodity fiction is our life experience, now subordinated to the market and turned into "behavioral surplus." Zuboff describes the enclosure of human life, like the enclosures of land. Behavioral surplus is "expropriated from the experiential realities of human beings whose bodies, thoughts and feelings are as virgin and blameless as nature's once plentiful meadows and forests before they fell to the market dynamic."[20] As our behavior is turned into a commodity we become "exiles from our own behavior, denied access to or control over knowledge derived from its dispossession by others for others."[21] As enclosed land has become the only option we can imagine, we have allowed the theft of our experiences to become commonplace. This is a relatively easy endeavor for corporations given that we cannot see or perceive it happening.

The Products

When it comes to big data, social media, and other free products on the internet, a common phrase is "if it's free, you're the product"—but Zuboff argues that human beings are better described as murdered and "abandoned carcass[es]" in the processes initiated by surveillance capitalists.[22] Once human beings are dispossessed of their experience, the behavioral surplus data is put into machine intelligence and analytic tools to create "prediction products." Therefore, while concerns about data privacy have some warrant, they are not the primary issue here since surveillance capitalists do not sell individual user data. Rather, user data is the raw input for analytic models that create the predictions products surveillance capitalists sell. The goal of such products is to "forecast what we will feel, think, and do: now, soon, and later" in order to minimize risk and increase certainty for those who buy them.[23]

The ability to minimize risk and increase certainty can be illustrated with the example of Google Ads, where surveillance capitalism was originally developed. This is also a useful example because Google Ads are heavily utilized by churches and other non-profits since Google offers up to

19. Zuboff, *Age of Surveillance Capitalism*, 99.
20. Zuboff, *Age of Surveillance Capitalism*, 100.
21. Zuboff, *Age of Surveillance Capitalism*, 100.
22. Zuboff, *Age of Surveillance Capitalism*, 377.
23. Zuboff, *Age of Surveillance Capitalism*, 96.

$10,000 a month in free ads via in-kind grants to qualifying non-profits.[24] For context, Google Ads appear when a user searches in Google or interacts on other Google affiliated outlets across the internet. These ads are generated and targeted to the user based on the behavioral surplus gathered across a wide range of platforms, which are used to generate profiles with machine learning tools to ensure that users only see an ad if Google deems it is relevant based on a user's behavioral profile.[25] In turn, the advertiser only pays for the ad if the person who sees the ad actually clicks on it. Rather than spending a lot of money on someone who may or may not care about their ad, Google Ads allow advertisers to utilize individualized messages that reach targeted individuals most interested in their content. As a result, surveillance capitalists minimize the risk to an advertiser of paying for ads that reach those who do not want to see them, and increases the probability of finding people who want to see their ads and will respond to them.[26] With such affordable benefits, why waste time and energy considering the costs?

The Marketplace

The marketplace for these prediction products started with Google in online advertising, but as this became successful, Google began expanding their collection of behavioral surplus outside the digital sphere. Then the market expanded beyond Google and online advertising. Now, as the desire for prediction grows, the need to extract more data shifts from the online world to the offline world. For example, think about a smartwatch, the extensive IT system in a new car, or the internet-connected devices in a person's so-called smart home. The primary goal for the companies selling these technologies is not convenience for the people buying them. The primary goal is gathering behavioral surplus to increase the predictive capability of their tools.[27] Consider the Nest thermostat, owned by Google since 2018. Zuboff recounts, "Nest's apps can gather data from other

24. "Google Grants" (https://www.google.com/grants/), accessed February 18, 2022. ChurchMarketing.is is one example of a church marketing service that offers consulting to help churches take advantage of these Google grants. They also offer social media management and Facebook advertising management.

25. Zuboff, *Age of Surveillance Capitalism*, 79.

26. Zuboff, *Age of Surveillance Capitalism*, 96.

27. Zuboff, *Age of Surveillance Capitalism*, 131.

connected products such as cars, ovens, fitness trackers, and beds."[28] Of course, Nest and these related apps have each of their own terms and conditions and "privacy policies," and one implicitly agrees to these terms to use these products and apps. However, according to two scholars who reviewed these policies, "Were one to enter into the Nest ecosystem of connected devices and apps . . . the purchase of a single home thermostat would entail the need to review nearly a thousand so-called contracts."[29] Practically speaking, when have *you* ever read through the entire end-user agreement for the latest technology device you purchased, unboxed, and started using? Technology companies are wagering that most people answer the question in the same way most people reading this book will: never.

The Church in the Desert

Many churches participate in surveillance capitalism in a multitude of ways, from simply creating and using Facebook pages, livestreaming on Facebook and YouTube, to employing Facebook and Google Ads, or the use of mobile apps for prayer that collect and employ user data in a variety of ways. Others have more formal partnerships and are testing and developing unique products with Facebook, which has a director for global faith partnerships who is also a nondenominal minister. The details of those partnerships are covered by non-disclosure agreements, but at a 2021 summit, faith leaders gathered and shared testimonies about how "Facebook helped them grow during the pandemic."[30] In at least one respect, then, some churches appear to be thriving in the desert.

At this point, I want to be careful not to shun technology altogether. The emergency lockdowns of the pandemic presented real challenges and needs for churches to connect, and disability communities are often well served when we are forced to creatively reimagine centralized Sunday gatherings, an expression that has often excluded the disabled,[31] and offer

28. Zuboff, *Age of Surveillance Capitalism*, 6.

29. Zuboff, *Age of Surveillance Capitalism*, 7.

30. Dias, "Facebook's Next Target."

31. Brock, *Disability*, provides a helpful account of how churches have practically and theologically marginalized disability communities and how churches can be more welcoming. Schmidt, *Virtual Communion*, argues that it is possible to create real community on the internet. In that case, we might ask with Ellul, what kinds of new technology are needed to create virtual community according to the eschatological reality of the kingdom of God? Is that possible? Ellul, "Technology and the Gospel," 114.

remote options. However, focusing here on surveillance capitalism and the situation of the church in the desert is an opportunity for theological reflection. It is explicable why many have turned to technique in an emergency, but such explicability should not prevent us from critically evaluating these methods moving forward. As the standard forms of gathering for church were stripped away and the dominant ways many people defined *church* was upended, there was and is a chance to reimagine church that has not always existed primarily or only as a Sunday morning gathering. From my perspective, the dust has not yet settled in the desert, and Ellul can help us consider both the dust and the desert.

With the above in view, I want to look more closely at Ellul's account of Israel's time in the desert following the Exodus to help us consider how churches' uses of surveillance capitalism as a technique accords with life in the desert. Ellul calls the entrance to the desert from Egypt the "entrance into both liberty and insecurity."[32] Again, the desert is an ambiguous and arduous place, so how do God's people survive in such a barren place? Ellul answers, "What makes living in the desert possible is the active presence of God. In his proximity, God on the one hand gives food . . . and on the other he shows the way. But in all that there is never anything constrained or obligatory; the only thing in which [people are] called to trust is the presence of God, as the pillar of fire and the pillar of cloud indicate."[33] What, then, is God's presence like? The philosopher Jeremy Bentham argued that panoptic surveillance simply replicated what God already did[34]—what about surveillance capitalism? How does the watching and presence of surveillance capitalism compare to the presence and knowledge of God?

I want to make two comparisons. The first comparison is Ellul's description of God's presence in the desert and the logic of surveillance capitalism that I have just outlined, and it aligns clearly with Ellul's critique of technology. In the second comparison I ask what kind of knowledge grounds God's presence and action, and compare the answer to this question with the knowledge generated by surveillance capitalists. To do this, I will look at God's self-revelation in Exodus 34.

32. Ellul, "The Desert," 15.

33. Ellul, "The Desert," 16.

34. See Lyon, "Surveillance and the Eye of God," for an analysis of Bentham's use of Psalm 139.

Power and Control in the Dark

Surveillance capitalists offer organizations attempts at "omniscience, control, and certainty."[35] Zuboff describes the new type of power created by surveillance capitalists as instrumentarian power. Instrumentarian power includes the "instrumentation and instrumentalization of behavior for the purposes of modification, prediction, monetization, and control." The instrumentation is essentially all the technology and technique wrapped up in surveillance capitalism. The instrumentalization is the effect, "The social relations that orient the puppet masters to human experience as surveillance capital wields the machines to transform us into the means to others' market ends."[36] In the end, Zuboff says "Machine processes replace human relationships so that certainty can replace trust."[37] Considering the church in the desert, we can see that surveillance capitalists offer the church the means to power, control, and certainty in a time of uncertainty.[38] With this power available, "The only remaining rule is that 'everything that can be done, ought to be done.'"[39] As the church follows this rule, we are utilizing tools that give us the ability to predict, manage, control—and yes, in many cases monetize—the human beings in our local bodies and our communities.

While these tools are seen as a means to discipleship and ministry, they are also a means of survival. They enable research, tracking, and measurement so we can streamline and optimize the ways we communicate with people for our intended goals, and that in turn shapes the goals we have so that they can be measured by techniques. As churches endeavor to serve human beings through the tools offered by surveillance capitalists, the very people they intend to serve are instrumentalized and become objects of the technique[40]—both for the church and for the broader capitalist system. However, Ellul writes, "The presence of God [in the desert] contradicts human expectations . . . and brings about the essential interruption: in

35. Zuboff, *Age of Surveillance Capitalism*, 383.

36. Zuboff, *Age of Surveillance Capitalism*, 352.

37. Zuboff, *Age of Surveillance Capitalism*, 351.

38. "Since the beginning of the technological era (eighteenth century in western history) technology of every kind has had only one aim, namely, the multiplication of means of power." Ellul, "Technology and the Gospel," 113.

39. Ellul, "Power of Technique and the Ethics of Non-Power," 244.

40. Ellul, *Presence in the Modern World*, 40.

human planning the desert closes in, whereas in God, it is liberty."[41] With the human imagination, the desert can feel like death and despair, it closes in on us and we cling to how we can manage, plan, and carry on based on what we know; with God, the desert brings liberation and liberates not only the human imagination, but the *entire* human being. Moreover, Ellul writes, "The presence of God appears like a contradiction in relation to the environment in which man finds himself: the pillar of fire shines at night, and the pillar of cloud creates the obscurity of the day."[42] In the desert, God's presence often shines brightest and most clearly when it is the darkest; when the way seems least clear.

This paradox, unexpectedness, and darkness are the opposite of control, management, and optimization, but they open possibilities in the desert. As Ellul highlights throughout his essay, an essential aspect of the desert experience is God's Word and revelation heard in the void. God speaks and creates, God reveals God's name to Moses, and God reveals to God's people, "I am the Lord your God, who brought you out of the land of Egypt" (Exod 20:2). These revelatory encounters are purposeful and they transform creation and creatures. Ellul writes, of the Exodus situation, "The experience of the desert takes place '*so that* you might know that I am the Lord your God' (Deut. 29:6) (NIV). Such an experience is both liberation, risk, initiative, obedience, and the inability to foresee, which engenders faith."[43] While we human beings are afraid of the dark and desperate to create our own light, the God of the desert invites us to know Godself in new ways as God leads us to freedom—even when it is dark and everything in the present and future in uncertain.

"Radical Indifference" as Pastoral Technique

Instrumentarian power creates a way of knowing that Zuboff labels as "radical indifference."[44] As surveillance capitalists and their technology observe, capture, and calculate for the sake of the market they "[remain] steadfastly indifferent to the meaning of that experience."[45] Zuboff de-

41. Ellul, "The Desert," 16.
42. Ellul, "The Desert," 16.
43. Ellul, "The Desert," 16.
44. Zuboff, *Age of Surveillance Capitalism*, 377.
45. Zuboff, *Age of Surveillance Capitalism*, 376–77.

scribes this knowledge as, "a form of *observation without witness*."[46] As human beings have become objects of their own means, Ellul writes that "Self-knowledge no longer leads to self-mastery; now self-knowledge leads to the enslavement of self. The means no longer discloses one's true image; it now reduces one to the condition of 'facsimile.'"[47] According to surveillance capitalism, human beings are recast as data simulacra for exploitation. One mobile marketer suggests that by opting in and providing more data, "The Truth will be present in everything. You'll know everything about yourself and your loved one."[48] But is such truth likely to set us free or enslave us? Is this observation and knowledge the same as God's presence and knowledge known by the people of God?

Ellul provides an answer to these questions when he recounts how God revealed God's name to Moses: "I am who I am" (Exod 3:14), and it is also in the desert that God makes a covenant with Moses and the people, revealing "I am the Lord your God, who brought you out of Egypt, out of the land of slavery You shall have no other gods before me" (Exod 20:2–3). Yet mere months after God rescued the Israelites from the land of Egypt, after God had provided manna and water from a rock, after God said, "You have seen what I did to the Egyptians, and how I bore you on eagles' wings and brought you to myself" (Exod 19:4), and after they saw God descend on Mt. Sinai in a dense cloud, the people got impatient waiting for Moses to return. They said to Aaron, "Come, make gods for us, who shall go before us" (Exod 32:1). And after they had completed the golden calf they said, "These are your gods, O Israel, who brought you out of the land of Egypt!" (Exod 32:5). God becomes angry, threatening to abandon Moses and the people on in their journey to the promised land, but Moses pleads with God saying, "How will anyone know that you are pleased with me and your people unless you go with us? What else will distinguish me and your people from all the other people on the face of the earth?" (Exod 20:16). God relents saying, "I will do the very thing you have asked, because I am pleased with you and I know you by name" (Exod 20:17). The encounter culminates in God revealing a glimpse of God's glory, and a new, fuller name to Moses. The first part of this name become a continual refrain in Israel's worship: "The Lord, the Lord, a God merciful and gracious, slow to anger, and abounding in steadfast love and faithfulness" (Exod 34:6).

46. Zuboff, *Age of Surveillance Capitalism*, 377.

47. Ellul, *Presence in the Modern World*, 49.

48. Turow, *Aisles Have Eyes*, 221.

This interaction alone indicates God's knowledge is not indifferent; there is no "observation without witness." God is intimately, emotionally involved with the lives of God's people, God hears, sees, responds. God knows them by name. And despite the unfaithfulness of the people God reaffirms the covenant revealing a key aspect of God's character foundational to the identity of God's people: *hesed*.[49]

Hesed is famously hard to translate from the Hebrew. In the NRSV it is "steadfast love," and in other translations we find "unfailing love," "lovingkindness," "loyalty," or any other number of words. Though humans can exhibit *hesed*, God's loyalty and steadfast love is distinct in a number of ways, including that it is "abounding" and "endures forever." It is abounding in that it relates to God's forgiveness. Despite the unfaithfulness and disloyalty of God's people, God continues to be loyal allowing the relationship, identity, and being of the people to continue, such as in this incident.[50] This love and loyalty only exists and is demonstrated within relationship, it is not a static quality but action-oriented.[51] This can be seen clearly in how *hesed* is used in the Psalms: divine love and loyalty is "manifest as help in need."[52] For example, Psalm 57:3 reads,

> He will send from heaven and save me,
> he will put to shame those who trample on me. *Selah*
> God will send forth his steadfast love and his faithfulness.

In Psalm 33:18–22, we see this steadfast love linked to the "eye of the Lord" and a reason why God's people trust and hope in God:

> Truly the eye of the Lord is on those who fear him,
> on those who hope in his steadfast love,
> to deliver their soul from death,
> and to keep them alive in famine.
> Our soul waits for the Lord;
> he is our help and shield.
> Our heart is glad in him,
> because we trust in his holy name.
> Let your steadfast love, O Lord, be upon us,
> even as we hope in you.

49. Sakenfeld, *Faithfulness in Action*, 40.
50. Sakenfeld, *Faithfulness in Action*, 49.
51. Sakenfeld, *Faithfulness in Action*, 3, 41.
52. Sakenfeld, *Faithfulness in Action*, 84.

We can consider Bentham's references to Psalm 139 in this context. While Bentham highlights the inability of the psalmist to escape the gaze of God, we can see that the psalmist is not disturbed or afraid of this, but rather is comforted to be continually in God's presence because it is a presence that provides care.

The people of God know themselves to be created and sustained by God's continuous action in history. From the time God saw them under the calculating, exploitative gaze of the Egyptian slaveholders and brought them out of bondage and provided for them in the desert, and onward, God's knowledge is not only *not indifferent*, but God's love shows a particular concern for the poor, marginalized, and oppressed.[53] This is the knowledge, presence, and sight that the people of God experience, trust, and praise. It is a knowledge grounded in steadfast love and mercy that hears, sees, and responds. Though we wander and forget, God is faithful. And though we wander, we also—by God's grace—remember to love actively rather than indifferently observe.

Conclusion: A Call to Non-power and Remembering

The church's use of tools provided by surveillance capitalists demonstrates the temptation of the desert articulated by Ellul, which is to take the means to the end of existence into our own hands: "The wilderness is therefore the place where temptation is revealed to be exactly what it is: that is, the incitement for [human beings] to take for [themselves] what God wants to give [them] and to use [their] own means and strength . . . to do what God has, in fact, given [them] to do."[54] Surveillance capitalism is a governing force in the trajectory of marketing practices designed to know and influence people personally, and when we examine this trajectory, it is striking to see how the practices attempt to approximate a spiritual discernment.[55] Yet, the church has and confesses the Spirit at work in the world and in the lives of the human beings in the body of Christ.

Why, then, are so many churches clinging to control, trying to see, predict, and manage with technologies like surveillance capitalism? Just

53. In *The Common Gaze*, Eric Stoddart argues for an ethic of surveillance and data gathering based on God's preferential option for the poor.

54. Ellul, "The Desert," 21.

55. I have made this point extensively in *Marketing and Christian Proclamation in Theological Perspective*.

as the Israelites had been freed from the Egyptians and kept wanting to return, longing for some sense of stability, many churches are wandering in a wasteland and worshipping the golden calf of economic rationality whose power and knowledge leads to slavery. Paraphrasing Psalm 135, without careful theological reflection we are likely to become like our idols, always observing without witnessing, hearing without listening, and calculating without knowing. Not only will the church become unable to truly know and hear each other, but as Ellul makes clear, we will be unable to hear God, to hear the new revelation God has for the church in this wilderness.

For Ellul, to hear the Word of God in the desert, to be healed of our alienation, and to discover a new way forward, will require churches to give up the power they have. "Our experience with the power of technique has led us to discover the absence of meaning . . . and the rediscovery of meaning is conditional upon the choice of non-power."[56] Therefore, "Given that the almost unlimited means at our disposal permit almost unlimited action, *we must choose, a priori, non-intervention each time there is uncertainty about the global and long-term effects of whatever actions are to be undertaken.*"[57] More specifically, churches that have power ought to choose non-power because Christ chose non-power.[58] Though many churches have the power to use the tools of surveillance capitalism, they must choose not to use them and wait for the Word of God in the desert they find themselves in today. Only God's Word can bring about transformation in the desert, and though the wait can be agonizing, the promise is certain and the work of God is always a movement from slavery to liberation. Because the "subordination of the spiritual to technical means . . . is the full stop placed before all [real] revolutionary possibility,"[59] the choice of non-power in the desert must be part of what Ellul calls a "revolutionary stance" in the modern world. But it is from the place of waiting and relying on the Word in the desert, so that "the *seeds of a new civilization* may spring up."[60] As Isaiah 43 admonishes while God's people were in the wilderness of exile,

> I am the Lord, your Holy One,
>   the Creator of Israel, your King.
> Thus says the Lord,

56. Ellul, "Power of Technique and the Ethics of Non-Power," 246.
57. Ellul, "Power of Technique and the Ethics of Non-Power," 245–46.
58. Ellul, "Technology and the Gospel," 113–14.
59. Ellul, *Presence in the Modern World*, 49.
60. Ellul, *Presence in the Modern World*, 38.

> who makes a way in the sea,
> a path in the mighty waters,
> who brings out chariot and horse,
> army and warrior;
> they lie down, they cannot rise,
> they are extinguished, quenched like a wick:
> Do not remember the former things,
> or consider the things of old.
> I am about to do a new thing;
> now it springs forth, do you not perceive it? (Isa 43:15–19)

How might we live in the desert as a place where we can hear Word of God? As the verses above in Isaiah 43 encourage: remember who your God is, remember what God has done for you, and be on the lookout for the new thing. *Remembering* became a consistent theme of God's people after their desert experience in Exodus. In the book of Deuteronomy, Moses repeatedly encourages the Israelites to remember what God did for them when God delivered them from Egypt and led them through the wilderness. "Make them known to your children and your children's children," God says (Deut 4:9). The Israelites learned that it is easy to forget God, and yet God is still faithful because God does not forget Israel. God is always present, hearing, responding, providing, guiding, and speaking. Thus Moses' reminder in Deuteronomy: remember! The Psalms are full of this refrain, "We will tell to the coming generation the glorious deeds of the Lord, and his might, and the wonders he has done . . . so that they should set their hope in God, and not forget the works of God, but keep his commandments" (Ps 78:4, 7). Dietrich Bonhoeffer echoes these sentiments in his meditation on Psalm 119: "Remembering and the repetition of what has been learned is a daily, necessary exercise. . . . Faith and obedience live out of remembrance and repetition. Remembrance becomes the power of the present because it is the living God who has acted for me once and assures me of that today."[61] While we wait in the desert, we can be confident of God's love, loyalty, healing, and deliverance. We do not need to take things into our own hands, clinging to power and control for the sake of survival and certainty. God's Word is clear and transformative. We can sing along with the psalmist and the people of God in history of his faithful action and steadfast love that endure forever:

61. Bonhoeffer, *Theological Education Underground*, 518.

O give thanks to the Lord, for he is good,
  for his steadfast love endures forever.
O give thanks to the God of gods,
  for his steadfast love endures forever.
O give thanks to the Lord of lords,
  for his steadfast love endures forever;
who alone does great wonders,
  for his steadfast love endures forever;
who by understanding made the heavens,
  for his steadfast love endures forever;
who spread out the earth on the waters,
  for his steadfast love endures forever;
who made the great lights,
  for his steadfast love endures forever;
the sun to rule over the day,
  for his steadfast love endures forever;
the moon and stars to rule over the night,
  for his steadfast love endures forever;
who struck Egypt through their firstborn,
  for his steadfast love endures forever;
and brought Israel out from among them,
  for his steadfast love endures forever;
with a strong hand and an outstretched arm,
  for his steadfast love endures forever;
who divided the Red Sea in two,
  for his steadfast love endures forever;
and made Israel pass through the midst of it,
  for his steadfast love endures forever;
but overthrew Pharaoh and his army in the Red Sea,
  for his steadfast love endures forever;
who led his people through the wilderness,
  for his steadfast love endures forever;
who struck down great kings,
  for his steadfast love endures forever;
and killed famous kings,
  for his steadfast love endures forever;
Sihon, king of the Amorites,
  for his steadfast love endures forever;
and Og, king of Bashan,
  for his steadfast love endures forever;
and gave their land as a heritage,
  for his steadfast love endures forever;

a heritage to his servant Israel,
  for his steadfast love endures forever.
It is he who remembered us in our low estate,
  for his steadfast love endures forever;
and rescued us from our foes,
  for his steadfast love endures forever;
who gives food to all flesh,
  for his steadfast love endures forever.
O give thanks to the God of heaven,
  for his steadfast love endures forever.

In the desert, the Word of God reminds us that we are watched over and cared for by the liberating God of Abraham, Isaac, and Jacob. But it is difficult, near impossible to remember—let alone hear and respond to—this Word if we are trying to watch and manage ourselves with powerful technologies.

Bibliography

Barna, George. *Marketing the Church: What They Never Taught You About Church Growth.* Colorado Springs: Navpress, 1988.

Bonhoeffer, Dietrich. *Theological Education Underground, 1937–1940.* Edited by Victoria J. Barnett. Translated by Victoria J. Barnett et al. Minneapolis: Fortress, 2011.

Brock, Brian. *Disability: Living into the Diversity of Christ's Body.* Grand Rapids, MI: Baker Academic, 2021.

Dias, Elizabeth. "Facebook's Next Target: The Religious Experience." *New York Times*, June 25, 2021. Accessed February 18, 2022. https://www.nytimes.com/2021/07/25/us/facebook-church.html.

Ellul, Jacques. "Technology and the Gospel." *International Review of Mission* 66, no. 262 (1977).

———. "The Power of Technique and the Ethics of Non-Power," 1980, Folder 34, Box: 20, Folder: 34. Jacques Ellul Papers, SC–016. Buswell Library Special Collections,

———. *Presence in the Modern World.* Translated by Lisa Richmond. Eugene, OR: Cascade Books, 2016.

Erickson, Amy J. *Ephraim Radner, Hosean Wilderness, and the Church in the Post-Christendom West: A Dialogue on the Shape of Waiting.* Brill Studies in Systematic Theology 22. Leiden: Brill, 2020.

Hill, Emily Beth. *Marketing and Christian Proclamation in Theological Perspective.* Lanham, MD: Lexington, 2021.

Horsfield, Peter. *From Jesus to the Internet: A History of Christianity and Media.* Hoboken, NJ: Wiley-Blackwell, 2015.

Lyon, David. "Surveillance and the Eye of God." *Studies in Christian Ethics* 27, no. 1 (2014).

Rah, Soong-Chan. *Prophetic Lament: A Call for Justice in Troubled Times.* Downers Grove, IL: InterVarsity, 2015.

Sakenfeld, Katherine Doob. *Faithfulness in Action: Loyalty in Biblical Perspective.* Philadelphia: Fortress, 1985.

Silliman, Daniel. "Venture Capitalists See Profit in Prayer." *Christianity Today.* January 7, 2022. Accessed February 18, 2022. https://www.christianitytoday.com/news/2022/january/app-investment-prayer-bible-meditation-glorify-hallow.html.

Shakespeare, Lyndon. *Being the Body of Christ in the Age of Management.* Eugene, OR: Cascade Books, 2016.

Schmidt, Katherine. *Virtual Communion: Theology of the Internet and the Catholic Sacramental Imagination.* Lanham, MD: Fortress Academic, 2020.

Stoddart, Eric. *The Common Gaze: Surveillance and the Common Good.* London, UK: SCM Press, 2021.

Turow, Joseph. *The Aisles Have Eyes: How Retailers Track Your Shopping, Strip Your Privacy, and Define Your Power.* New Haven, CT: Yale University Press, 2017.

Wright, Christopher J. H. *"Here Are Your Gods": Faithful Discipleship in Idolatrous Times.* Downers Grove, IL: IVP Academic, 2020.

Zuboff, Shoshana. *The Age of Surveillance Capitalism: The Fight for a Human Future at the New Frontier of Power.* New York, NY: PublicAffairs, 2020.

Chapter Five

Wilderness Theology and Degrowth

Jason Hudson

In his exploration of the relationship between Christianity and sensuality, Søren Kierkegaard claims, "It is self-evident that what is to be excluded always pre-exists what excludes it, even if in another sense it first comes into existence through its exclusion."[1] The same relationship exists between wilderness and technique. Wilderness precedes technique though the latter gives rise to the concept of the former *and* excludes it through technological modes of mastery and commodification. Jacques Ellul saw this relationship between technique and nature as one of the "obvious characteristics" of technique. He explains,

> Technique is opposed to nature. Art, artifice, artificial: technique as art is the creation of an artificial system. . . . The world that is being created by the accumulation of technical means is an artificial world and hence radically different from the natural world. It destroys, eliminates, or subordinates the natural world, and does not follow this world to restore itself or even to enter into a symbiotic relation with it. The two worlds obey different imperatives, different directives, and different laws which have nothing in common.[2]

For Ellul, technique, in one motion, defines nature's contours and reduces it to a technologically communicable form. This is achieved through the

1. Kierkegaard, *Either/Or*, 73.
2. Ellul, *Technological Society*, 79.

aspect of technique that Ellul calls "self-augmentation"[3] as the frontier between nature and technique demarcates the scope of nature and technique expands its colonization over nature.

This essay explores the antagonism between technique and nature as expounded in Jacques Ellul's essay "The Desert" and seeks to bring key aspects of Ellul's wilderness theology to bear on a Christian approach to degrowth economics. Degrowth is a relatively new and marginal approach to economics and ecology that, at its core, is concerned with antagonisms between nature and technique. The convergences and divergences between Ellul's thinking and the current discourse about degrowth make it a fitting case study. While Ellul's thought aligns with degrowth's desire to impose limitations on the scale and use of technologies by submitting them to standards that resist mechanization and commodification, his distaste for bureaucracy, centralized power, and planned economies puts him at odds with many current degrowth proposals. Ellul's insistence that Christians live distinctly, responsive to the conditions of each unique situation, provides a helpful corrective to the draconian and politically implausible proposals of many degrowth advocates. To facilitate such a Christian lifestyle in today's "human desert,"[4] I suggest that a spiritual discipline of wilderness is needed to re-wild the church and prepare Christians to be a re-wilding presence to break up the ossified and banal colonies of technique.

Growth and Degrowth as a Case of Technique and Wilderness[5]

In "The Desert," Ellul shows the antagonism between technique and wilderness to be fundamentally about power. He writes, "The desert is the

3. Ellul, *Technological Society*, 85–94.

4. Ellul, "The Desert," 23. "The Human Desert" is a section heading in Ellul's essay with no content. It is provocative and suggestive, but apart from brief preliminary notes, we must speculate what Ellul might have meant by this phrase. Here it is used to mean the technological desert, the city as desert. Simply, the conditions Ellul describes as desert are present today in techno-saturated civilizations.

5. Ellul uses the terms desert and wilderness interchangeably in his essay, seeming to prefer desert when discussing biblical texts and wilderness when discussing the theological implications of his reading. In this essay, I will use *nature* as the most expansive term denoting all uncultivated creation. I will use *wilderness* as the umbrella term that includes the particular wilderness of desert, but more generally refers to all of the uncultivated places in which people experience both the provision and grace of God and

place where the world's power shows itself to be powerless."[6] Because of this technological impotence, "the entrance into the desert is very clearly the entrance into both liberty and insecurity."[7] Liberty and insecurity are inseparable in the desert because it is the place of spiritual encounter unbuffered by technique. In a corollary study, Ellul's exegesis of Genesis 4 reveals that Cain's inability to accept such vulnerability drove him to build the first city. "Cain is completely dissatisfied with the security granted to him by God," Ellul writes, "and so he searches out his own security."[8] Cain builds the city to provide his own protection, to reject God's presence, and to resist the condition of wilderness vulnerability. Ellul asserts, "The life of a powerful city is but a constant succession of revolts against God."[9] A dialectic emerges in which the technological orientation of the city is linked with power and control while the orientation of wilderness is linked with freedom and trust borne of powerlessness.[10]

These two modes of being are central to modern economics. Mainstream economic approaches espouse the necessity and desirability of GDP growth as self-evident. A good economy is a growing economy, so the assumption goes. Growth economies correspond to technique and the city[11] and they are extractive and abusive toward nature. Growth economies continue the antagonism between technique and nature through mechanization, commodification, and the homogeneous application of exploitative technologies. The relationship between technology, growth economies, and the abuse of nature is on clear display in land use sectors of the economy. In industrial food production, for example, technique has wrought ideologies of growth—what degrowth activists call *growthism*—that engender

spiritual temptation, where the technological mediators that stand between humanity and nature are stripped away, leaving only the vulnerable individual with a choice: to receive the gift of God by faith or to fold to the temptation of technique.

6. Ellul, "The Desert," 15.

7. Ellul, "The Desert," 15.

8. Ellul, *Meaning of the City*, 4.

9. Ellul, *Meaning of the City*, 50.

10. Ellul's work is fundamentally dialectic in nature, though scholars differ on exactly what the dialectic components of Ellul's thought are at the highest level. Cf. Goddard, *Living the Word, Resisting the World*. Chapter 2 reviews and critiques the major approaches to Ellul's dialectic before arguing that communion and rupture are the "interpretive key" that "enables a coherent account to be given of Ellul's wider theology and ethic" (60).

11. Ellul, *Meaning of the City*, 151. Here Ellul links technique and the city to economics.

technological expansion as well as the augmentation of machinery. These expansions have had double effect of homogenizing agricultural techniques and reducing the fertility of landscapes. The search for the 'one best way' in agriculture has led to unique landscapes being treated the same as every other, as the machine cannot account for the particular eccentricities of places. The result of these, and other, technological approaches to food production has led to a crisis of fertility. These aspects of industrial food production reveal that technique's mode of control through technological power seeks to tame the wildness of unique places and force them into standardized and atomized fodder for technique.[12]

Against the alliance of technique and growthism, degrowth economics embraces limitation and submits technological expansion to what it sees to be higher goods. Degrowth is the English translation of the French *décroissance*. The translation *degrowth* is favored over more literal options like decrease or reduce because of a desire to avoid affiliation with recession or austerity. Degrowth is not a slowdown of the economy as is; rather it is a ground up rethinking of the economy to account for ecological and natural limitations. According to George Kallis, "Degrowth signifies a society with a smaller metabolism, but more importantly, a society with a metabolism that has a different structure and serves new functions. Degrowth does not call for doing less of the same. The objective is not to make an elephant leaner, but to turn an elephant into a snail."[13] Christian Roy calls proponents of degrowth, "Naysayers to the established religion of endless growth that is the self-evident common tenet of all other ideologies, whether right, left, or even mainstream ecological."[14] Roy also demonstrates that Ellul and his friend Bernard Charbonneau were early proponents of the philosophies that later informed degrowth.[15] Acknowledging their influence on the ecology movements in France, Ellul remarks, "[Charbonneau's] love and his concern for nature led him to the now popular concept that 'one cannot pursue infinite development within a finite world.' Charbonneau said it in 1944."[16] Additionally, Ellul aligns with advocates of degrowth by demonstrating that technique's extractive power over nature is abusive

12. For Ellul's consideration of the relationship between agriculture and technique, cf. Ellul, *Technological Society*, 106–10, 116.

13. D'Alisa et al., *Degrowth*, 4.

14. Roy, "Jacques Ellul and Bernard Charbonneau," 52.

15. Roy, "Jacques Ellul and Bernard Charbonneau," 52.

16. Ellul and Garrigou-Lagrange, *In Season, Out of Season*, 143.

and reductive. According to Ellul, technique supplants and commodifies nature, reducing it to what Martin Heidegger calls "standing-reserve" or "*Bestand*."[17] Technological power, in its desire to master, control, and tame wilderness strips it of mystery. According to Ellul,

> Technique worships nothing, respects nothing. It has a single role: to strip off externals, to bring everything to light, and by rational use to transform everything into means. . . . Science brings to the light of day everything man had believed sacred. Technique takes possession of it and enslaves it. The sacred cannot resist. Science penetrates to the great depths of the sea to photograph the unknown fish of the deep. Technique captures them, hauls them up to see if they are edible— but before they arrive on deck they burst. And why should technique not act thus? It is autonomous and recognizes as barriers only the temporary limits of its action.[18]

Even the wildest peripheries of earth are exploited and commodified under the influence of technique's power. The once sacrosanct is exposed as mundane and banal by technique.

The foundational convergence between Ellul and degrowth is the desire to emasculate technological power by submitting it to the higher good of human and ecological flourishing. By subordinating market growth to evaluative metrics that include dignity, welfare, conviviality, elegance, and happiness, degrowth transgresses technique's dominant ideologies. In a passage that singularly highlights Ellul's alignment with degrowth, he writes, "In economy, aiming at growth means trying to produce more cement, more iron, or more wheat. Aiming at development means looking for the most balanced and least harmful economic structure, recognizing the value of the statement 'small is beautiful,' and achieving higher quality in consumption."[19] Before moving past this point, a clarification is needed.

Despite his criticism of technological exploitation, Ellul does not advocate for the sacralization of nature. Rather, he understands that technological secularization is a farce. He asserts as a law of the sacred that, "when there is a process of desacralization, the very factor that produces it gives

17. Heidegger, *Question concerning Technology*. Ellul does not reference Heidegger in this regard, but the category of standing-reserve is helpful to understand the reductionistic influence of technique over nature.

18. Ellul, *Technological Society*, 142.

19. Ellul, *Perspectives on Our Age*, 79.

birth to a new form of the sacred."[20] Elsewhere he clarifies, "Man cannot live without the sacred. Therefore he transfers his sense of the sacred to the very thing which has destroyed its former object: to technique itself."[21] Consequently, wilderness is sacrificed to the sacred of technique. Because technique becomes sacred, all other standards or metrics of value are submitted to it. The wildness of wilderness is capricious, spontaneous, and useless; these are the inefficiencies that technique cannot accept. Ellul's view of the sacred brings the antagonism between wilderness and technique into a new light to reveal that the temptation presented by technique to master or tame wilderness is at its core a matter of worship and idolatry.

Temptation in the Wilderness

In "The Desert," Ellul notes in brief what he has expounded elsewhere, that the three temptations of Christ in the desert are common to all temptation and at root are the temptation to take up the means of power: to use economic, political, and spiritual power to achieve what God has already given.[22] "The wilderness," Ellul contends, "is therefore the place where temptation is revealed to be . . . the incitement for man to take for himself what God wanted to give him and to use his own means and strength (Ishmael) to do what God has, in fact, given him to do."[23] For Ellul, wilderness brings this core spiritual reality, which is obscured by technological society, into stark relief. Therefore, wilderness puts the same question to all humanity: will you patiently and peacefully receive the gifts of God, or will you violently take what God have freely and graciously given because you are impatient?

The most direct biblical parallel to Jesus's desert temptation is the temptation of Adam and Eve. Although Ellul does not name the Edenic temptation among his biblical cases of desert, the conditions are consistent with what he calls desert elsewhere; the prelapsarian humans experience the presence and grace of God, they hear the Word of God, and they are tempted by the serpent. Ellul shows the Edenic temptation to be, in essence,

20. Ellul, *Subversion of Christianity*, 54.

21. Ellul, *Technological Society*, 143. In his later works he will nuance what he says here by tracing the sacred along "the twofold axis of 'technolgy/sex' and nation-state/revolution." Cf. Ellul, *Subversion of Christianity*, 54; Ellul, *New Demons*, 70–87.

22. Ellul, *Ethics of Freedom*, 52–61; Ellul, *If You Are the Son of God*, 55–94.

23. Ellul, "The Desert," 21.

the same as Jesus's desert temptation—to take by their own means what has already been given by God. Genesis 1:27 shows that the likeness to God has been given. So, the temptation to eat the fruit with its promise of being like God (Gen 3:5) is not a matter of ends but of means. The Holy Spirit leads Jesus into the wilderness to experience the same temptation. Ellul writes, "The devil suggests that Jesus simply accomplish what God sent him to do! Yet Jesus refuses. He refuses his own temptation to wield this universal power rapidly, to wield it himself by taking it."[24] Elsewhere Ellul connects these parallel temptation stories: "The approach of Jesus is the exact opposite of that of Adam. Adam wanted to be equal to God. It was not enough to be his image, to be the steward in charge of all his goods, to talk to God face to face. He wanted to be an absolute master and he snatched creation out of God's hands."[25] Adam and Eve follow a pattern that recurs throughout Scripture: see, desire, and take. It is often the same for Adam and Eve's descendants: we see, we desire, we take, and we lose sight of the ends in the dizzying frenzy of means aimed at achieving what has already been given by a gracious God.

Wilderness as Spiritual Discipline

To this point, I have suggested that the antagonistic relationship between technique and wilderness is fundamentally about two modes of being. Technique relates to the world through power and desires to master or control nature, reducing creation to a mechanized, atomized, and commodified resource (*Bestand*). Wilderness, as an alternative mode of being, embraces freedom and vulnerability, and, in wilderness the technological buffers between the human and spiritual world are thinned to allow for spiritual encounter, both demonic temptation and the Word of God. Finally, the parallel temptations of Adam and Eve and Jesus reveal that power, the animating spirit of technique, tempts humanity to take rather than receive what God has meant to be a gracious gift.

From this basis, I will turn to consider how the Spirit can lead modern Christians into the wilderness and then back to civilization as a rewilding presence and how this ethic of presence might inform a Christian approach to degrowth. Despite Ellul and Charbonneau's influence on the degrowth movement, much of the current discourse around degrowth is incompatible

24. Ellul, *If You Are the Son of God*, 65.

25. Ellul, *Ethics of Freedom*, 218.

with Ellul's thought. For example, "Contemporary degrowth movements and authors have emphasized systems change by focusing mostly on changing production relations or reducing resource throughputs."[26] This is a policy first approach that calls for a planned restructuring of major economies to be enforced by centralized authorities. While policy changes are undoubtedly necessary to address current ecological crises, many of the policy proposals advocated by degrowth activists are not politically viable and cannot be justly implemented. Wendell Berry highlights the problem quipping, "It is apparently easy to say that there are too many farmers, if one is not a farmer. This is not a pronouncement often heard in farm communities. . . . No agricultural economist has yet perceived that there are too many agricultural economists."[27] The chief question and the thorn in degrowth's side is: who decides which sectors of the economy must shrink and how can such a slowdown justly be achieved?

Some degrowth activists acknowledge that a policy heavy approach is inadequate. A recent article acknowledged the need, "To embody the transition [to degrowth] and its deeper meanings in a personal way."[28] The article also suggests a need for "deeper shifts in ideology and daily practices."[29] Responding to the need for daily practices and a more personal approach, I suggest in what follows that, regardless of the policies that may or may not come from world leaders, a spiritual discipline of wilderness is needed for the contemporary church to be a hopeful rewilding presence against the hopelessness of technological determinism and ecological catastrophe.

In "The Desert," Ellul highlights several aspects of desert that can be taken up as a spiritual practice. Though Ellul does not use the language of spiritual discipline or practice, this approach allows for meaningful engagement with degrowth which flips the topheavy, policy first approach upside down to emphasize a personal and distinctly Christian approach. The wilderness disciplines considered are not exhaustive but are meant to provoke further consideration and action that will lead to a distinctly Christian ethic of wild presence.

First, according to Ellul, "A rupture is needed, an abandon."[30] The first wilderness discipline is to cross the threshold from the security of the

26. EmboDegrowth Lab, "Embodying Degrowth."

27. Berry, *What Are People For?*, 123.

28. EmboDegrowth Lab, "Embodying Degrowth."

29. EmboDegrowth Lab, "Embodying Degrowth."

30. Ellul, "The Desert," 12.

city (metaphorical or literal)—the buffered realm of technique—and consciously enter the unknown wilderness. Jesus regularly left civilization and the crowds that followed him to enter the wilderness for times of prayer and solitude. The traverse into the wilderness was his *custom* (Luke 22:39). Christians, likewise, in order to be rewilded and to break free of the hardening determinism of technique must traverse the threshold into wilderness.

For Ellul, however, this is no romanticism; no trendy 'back to the land' movement. The traverse must not be commodified, politicized, or otherwise technological. A wilderness vacation in which one hopes to find renewal by getting 'in touch' with nature misses the mark. The mode of this kind of leisure or vacation remains thoroughly technological. The goal is extractive, and the vulnerability required for true wilderness is avoided. The difference is one of attention and not merely of danger or discomfort. In conversation with Madleine Garrigou-Lagrange, Ellul criticizes such commodified and facile encounters with nature. Regarding his opposition to the development of the Aquitaine coastal region, he says, "We contest the style of vacation of the guy who goes to the mountains or the seaside, goes skiing or motorboating for two weeks, and then leaves."[31] Against this kind of easy wilderness tourism, Ellul espouses his view that "nature is not only a place where one goes for a vacation, it is a world to discover, to penetrate, in company with its inhabitants."[32] While commodified nature is reduced to its aspects that are pleasurable or useful, true wilderness creates an encounter which puts a question to the one who experiences it; experience of true wilderness presents a risk. Wilderness is risky because it questions humanity, confronts us with mortality, and exposes technological impotence.

To preempt an obvious objection, traversing the wilderness is not a luxury available only to those who can afford to shop at REI and have plenty of vacation days and access to travel. We must dispel the illusion of pristine wilderness. As recent images of climbers waiting in line to reach the pinnacle of Mount Everest proves, pristine wilderness is a relic of a preindustrial past. Moreover, the presence of artificial chemicals called per- and polyfluoroalkyl substances (PFAS) in the earth's water system and in human and animal blood further reveals the extinction of untouched wilderness. On the other hand, wilderness can be experienced in urban environments and even in contemplation of the wildness of humanity. As Wendell Berry claims, "Our bodily life . . . is half wild. Perhaps it is more

31. Ellul and Garrigou-Lagrange, *In Season, Out of Season*, 151.

32. Ellul and Garrigou-Lagrange, *In Season, Out of Season*, 152.

than half wild, for it is dependent upon reflexes, instincts, and appetites that we do not cause or intend and that we cannot, or had better not, stop."[33] The traverse requires one to come consciously into the presence of wilderness wherever it is found. It is not, to be clear, simply a state of mind. It is, rather, an attentive presence with wilderness given the proper understanding that wilderness can be found even in the most technological metropolis. Like a weed breaking through the cracks in a concrete walkway, wilderness lurks, threatening to emerge and expose the fractures in technique's dominance over nature.

The second wilderness discipline is silence. Silence is often considered among the disciplines of Christian practice. However, for Ellul, the silence experienced in wilderness is distinct. Ellul notes an etymological link between desert (*midbar*) and God's word (*dabar*).[34] Yet, in the wilderness God's word "comes solely by grace."[35] Therefore, "the wilderness is the terrible place of total abandonment—with no guarantee that God is there."[36] Even though God's word "resonates in the desert,"[37] it is also a place where God's silence is thickened because the noise of technological distractions—"human technique"[38]—is hushed. It is precisely because God's Word is not present that it can come. The discipline of wilderness silence requires that one not come into the wilderness with an agenda. It requires resting and waiting in silent transparency before God. Wilderness silence relinquishes the technological modes of mastery and control. Nothing can be extracted from God. God is free and no technique can act upon God.[39] Therefore, the only recourse is to enter into wilderness silence and wait for the Word of God.

Wilderness silence leads to the third discipline: listening and discerning the Word of God. In the hushed stillness of wilderness one can hear the voice that resonates in the wilderness. With Elijah, we listen for God's whisper. As we seek wisdom for rewilding civilization, we hear God's word in the wilderness as an echo of God's primordial judgment, "It is very good" (Gen. 1:31). The wilderness that lives on the periphery of our societies are

33. Berry, "Preserving Wildness," in Berry, *Home Economics*, 139–40.

34. Ellul, "The Desert," 17.

35. Ellul, "The Desert," 20.

36. Ellul, "The Desert," 20.

37. Ellul, "The Desert," 10.

38. Ellul, *Technological Society*, 319–40.

39. Cf. Ellul, *Prayer and Modern Man*, 144–45.

schools for innovation that align with what Aldo Leopold calls "the base datums of normality." The wisdom to be learned from the wilderness of particular localities is, *what would nature do in this place if it were left alone?* In response to this wild wisdom, those seeking to innovate for degrowth must ask how the lessons of wilderness bear on what humans can and should do in a particular place.[40]

The Word of God sought in wilderness is the one that technique cannot accept. The Word submits technique to creation so that it might, "Follow this world to restore itself or even to enter into a symbiotic relation with it."[41] However, as Ellul explains, this is what technique cannot do. Therefore, the Word of God resonating in the wilderness is an exorcistic/ iconoclastic Word that strips technology of the spirit of technique. This is precisely the goal of degrowth activists who, following Ivan Illich,[42] seek the development of convivial technologies which are locally adapted and promote ecological and human wellbeing.[43]

The fourth wilderness discipline is Sabbath. Ellul notes that Israel came out of Egypt and entered the wilderness "to worship a God about whom they can say nothing."[44] Israel entered the wilderness to receive revelation from God, to be chosen by God, and to be fed by the hand of God. A key aspect of this revelation, as Walter Brueggemann among others, has shown was to reorient Israel as worshipers of a Sabbath-keeping God, against the "confiscatory gods who demand endless produce and who authorize endless systems of production that are, in principle, insatiable."[45] For Brueggemann the antagonism between Sabbath and the technological mode of economic growth is clear. He writes, "The way of mammon (capital, wealth) is the way of commodity that is the way of endless desire, endless productivity, and endless restlessness without any Sabbath."[46] He makes the connection to degrowth explicit by describing Sabbath as a way of resisting the demands and ideologies of the market economy. Sabbath, which was commanded for

40. Ellul emphatically opposes natural theology. Nonetheless, outside of an attempt to build a cataphatic theology based on wilderness observation, the ability to discern the wisdom of God's creation reflected in its wild state remains valid.

41. Ellul, *Prayer and Modern Man*, 89.

42. Illich, *Tools for Conviviality*.

43. Cf. Vetter, "Matrix of Convivial Technology."

44. Ellul, "The Desert," 30.

45. Brueggemann, *Sabbath as Resistance*, 14.

46. Brueggemann, *Sabbath as Resistance*, 16.

people, animals, and landscapes, is a buffer against technological reduction of everything to utility or commodity. Today, again, Christians must go into the wilderness to learn a subversive Sabbath which resists the ideologies of growth economies. In economic terms, the discipline of Sabbath is about accounting for the value of inutility.

Finally, the fifth discipline is to return to civilization. Ellul is critical of the desert fathers who fled Rome in the fourth and fifth centuries because they, "Went to the desert 'not only' to find purity, flee temptations, concentrate (flee distractions), but 'also' to stay. There is no desire to go back to the world afterwards."[47] Ellul notes that the Apostle Paul and Saint Augustine spend time in wilderness following their conversations, yet they return to "the world," to society. Likewise, Jesus demonstrated a regular rhythm of oscillation between wilderness retreat for seclusion and prayer and return to his disciples and ministry to the crowds.

Christian presence, so central for Ellul's understanding of the Christian vocation, is the result of this oscillation. Disciplines of wilderness restore a measure of wildness to the one who traverses the threshold into wilderness. Ellul says this about the effects of mechanized time on people's relationship to their own biology: "He was made to eat when he was hungry and to sleep when he was sleepy; instead, he obeys a clock. He was made to have contact with living things, and he lives in a world of stone. He was created with a certain essential unity, and he is fragmented by all the forces of the modern world."[48] After the mechanization of time, Ellul argues, "Life itself was measured by the machine; its organic functions obeyed the mechanical. Eating, working, and sleeping were at the beck and call of machinery. Time, which had been the measure of organic sequence, was broken and dissociated."[49] In the wilderness this mechanized relationship of the human person to his or her body and experience of time breaks down. Biological needs and natural rhythms are reintroduced. A measure of wildness is restored. For Ellul, this wild presence is central to the Christian mission. Ellul often appeals to John 3:8 to make this point: "The wind blows wherever it pleases. You hear its sound, but you cannot tell where it comes from or where it is going. So it is with everyone born of the Spirit."[50] Into a technological age in which

47. Ellul, "The Desert," 15.

48. Ellul, *Technological Society*, 325.

49. Ellul, *Technological Society*, 329.

50. For example, Ellul, *Subversion of Christianity*, 156.

steps, calories, minutes, friends, and 'likes' are counted, Christian presence injects wildness, non-quantifiable, even quixotic, useless pastimes.[51]

The wilding presence which pushed back against mechanization has direct implications for the development of technologies and how work is understood in a degrowth economy. For example, Ellul contends, "Local activities must be developed to the advantage of craftsmen, small businessmen, and farmers; neither the tourist's interests nor the so-called general interest of the economy should be put ahead of them."[52] Here Ellul resonates with Wendell Berry's view of economy as a ground up *oikonomika*, an economy that grows out of the needs and eccentricities of unique localities.

Eschatology—Enacting a Wilderness City

The oscillation described above creates the ethical dimension of Ellul's thinking. Christians, having been rewilded by the freedom and vulnerability of wilderness disciplines, return to live a wilderness-formed life in the city, to rupture the monotonous and deterministic modes of technique. To conclude this essay, I will explore the eschatological dimension of Christian presence, to suggest that the result of the oscillation between wilderness and civilization is the here and now foreshadowing of New Jerusalem, a garden city.

Ellul's eschatology clarifies how his wilderness theology relates to Christian vocation. He writes, God's "final promise is precisely that there will be no more desert, that the desert itself will become fertile."[53] Many Christians today err by way of the quietism of climate change denial on the basis of this promise. This is certainly a mistake. Although God promised Israel their own land, they were nevertheless taken into exile as a judgment for their idolatry. God's promises do not neuter God's judgment. Likewise, the promise that the deserts will be made fertile does not negate the realities of climate change or other ecological disaster as consequences of human action. In fact, it seems in close keeping with the patterns of Scripture that humanity would suffer ecological consequences—as a kind of exilic wondering—for their idolatrous joining with the machine to master the creation rather than to join with God in keeping and tilling it (Gen 2:15).

51. Cf. Ellul's "Meditation on Inutility," in Ellul, *Politics of God and the Politics of Man*, 190–99.

52. Ellul and Garrigou-Lagrange, *In Season, Out of Season*, 156.

53. Ellul, "The Desert," 11.

For Ellul, the Christian vocation to hope is precisely to enter the tension of the former promises of God and the current silence. Denial is not hope. Hope enters the reality of ecological catastrophe and nonetheless proclaims the faithfulness of God.

Ellul understands prayer to be a central ethical component of Christians who enter into the silent space between God's promise and fulfillment. This is the ethical component of wilderness silence. Christians enter the silence and contend with God in prayer. In response to ecological catastrophe, it is the role of Christians to accuse God in his silence and abandonment. Christians must insist—in a kind of prayer that Ellul calls combat[54]—that God remember God's promises. Christians go to the desert, to the reality of ecological existential desecration, and nonetheless prophesy that the deserts will become fertile and that resurrection is possible.

Despite Ellul often being misread as a pessimist, he does not suggest that Christians wait passively for the eschaton. Rather, Christians are to develop an eschaton shaped style of life. In Ellul's eschatology, the promise that the desert will be fertile does not produce quietism; it produces creativity, and a Christian lifestyle that is free from the determinisms of technique, free to live in the Holy Spirit, the church's animating force—not capricious but spontaneous, blowing here and there without condition or compulsion. In Ellul's scheme, Spirit-filled Christians freely devote themselves to creative attempts to live within God's eschatological vision—cultivating a world in which non-power fulfills the eschatological vision of peace and where alternative approaches to agriculture (permaculture, food forests, and urban agriculture, for example) bring about ecological flourishing in cities and deserts.

The relationship between human work and divine work in Ellul is complex but essential to understanding his theology. The desert is the place where humanity is stripped of power. Yet it is the place where humanity learns to trust God and live fully by God's provision. Nonetheless, according to Ellul "it is still man, by himself, who is called to cross the desert. His work is indispensable."[55] People must act. Human action alone is devoid of meaning until given one by the Word of God and God's appropriation of human artifice in the eschatological agrarian city. There is, however, no guarantee of this act of God's appropriation. As Ellul writes, there is "no

54. Ellul, *Prayer and Modern Man*, 139–78.

55. Ellul, "The Desert," 16.

guarantee that God is there. God comes solely by grace."[56] Stripped of the means of power and the spiritual certainty that God will intervene, humans must act.

The technological mode of power and control cannot accept this precarious position. Ellul, however, calls Christians to act despite uncertainty, to follow the way of Jesus who entered the desert to refuse the way of power and to receive from God what was given (Phil 2:6–11). Wilderness disciplines offer Christians a way between the quietism of denial and the anxiety of technique. Moreover, a Spirit born renewal of Christians who are like the wind in their wildness and freedom, who enter into the silence between God's promise and fulfillment, who discern the Word of God resonating in the wilderness, and who follow Christ in refusing the way of power is a potential groundswell for the hopes of degrowth.

I must confess skepticism. In a time when the church is increasingly divided, especially about matters with social or political implication, it is difficult to believe that such a move of the Spirit is possible. And in a time when the church is thoroughly technologized it is likely that any movement toward such wilderness disciplines will be commodified and marketed as a new church growth strategy. And yet, here in my own doubt is a case in point, for, "With man it is impossible, but not with God. For all things are possible with God" (Mark 10:27).

Bibliography

Berry, Wendell. *Home Economics: Fourteen Essays*. Berkeley: Counterpoint, 1987.

———. *What Are People For?* New York: North Point, 1990.

Brueggemann, Walter. *Sabbath as Resistance: Saying No to the Culture of Now*. Louisville: Westminster John Knox, 2017.

D'Alisa, Giacomo, et al. *Degrowth: A Vocabulary for a New Era*. New York: Routledge Taylor, & Francis Group, 2015.

Ellul, Jacques. *The Ethics of Freedom*. Translated by Geoffrey W. Bromiley. London: Mowbrays, 1976.

———. *If You Are the Son of God*. Translated by Anne-Marie Andreasson-Hogg. Eugene, OR: Cascade, 2014.

———. *The Meaning of The City*. Translated by Denis Pardee. Eugene, OR: Wipf & Stock, 2011.

———. *The New Demons*. Translated by C. Edward Hopkin. New York: Seabury, 1975.

———. *Perspectives on Our Age*. Edited by Willem H. Vanderburg. Translated by Canadian Broadcasting Corporation. Toronto: House of Anansi Press, 2004.

56. Ellul, "The Desert," 20.

———. *The Politics of God and the Politics of Man*. Translated by Geoffrey W. Bromiley. Grand Rapids: Eerdmans, 1972.

———. *Prayer and Modern Man*. Translated by C. Edward Hopkin. New York: Seabury, 1970.

———. *Subversion of Christianity*. Translated by Geoffrey W. Bromiley. Eugene, OR: Wipf & Stock, 2001.

———. *The Technological Society*. Translated by John Wilkinson. New York: Vintage 1964.

Ellul, Jacques, and Madeleine Garrigou-Lagrange. *In Season, Out of Season*. Translated by Lani K. Niles. San Francisco: Harper & Row, 1982.

The EmboDegrowth Lab. "Embodying Degrowth and Turning the Movement Inside Out." *Degrowth*, August 7, 2022. https://degrowth.info/en/blog/embodying-degrowth-and-turning-the-movement-inside-out.

Goddard, Andrew. *Living the Word, Resisting the World: The Life and Thought of Jacques Ellul*. Carlisle: Paternoster, 2002.

Heidegger, Martin. *The Question Concerning Technology*. Translated by William Lovitt. New York: HarperPerennial, 2013.

Illich, Ivan. *Tools for Conviviality*. New York: Harper & Row, 1973.

Kierkegaard, Søren. *Either/Or: A Fragment of Life*. Translated by Alastair Hannay. New York: Penguin Classics, 2004.

Roy, Christian. "Jacques Ellul and Bernard Charbonneau in French Surveys of the Degrowth Movement." *Ellul Forum* 65 (2020) 51–64.

Vetter, Andrea. "The Matrix of Convivial Technology—Assessing Technologies for Degrowth." *Journal of Cleaner Production* 197 (2018) 1778–86.

Chapter Six

Hearing the Void, Responding to the Voice

Ethics for Living and Dying in the Desert

Jacob Marques Rollison

If we see the image of a desert wasteland showing us something true about our present reality—if, in our overcrowded networks of lonely people, that Babel-esque conjunction of technical prowess and failed communication, we can discern a barrenness behind the light and sound; if being whatever we want to be has left us with no idea about how to be what we are; if we no longer recognize ourselves in our selfies, if we are sick of singing songs which, instead of translating our deepest cries, infect our memories and move our members in repetitive obedience to calculated commercial stimuli; and if, in the absence of words worth living and dying for, meaninglessness tracks us with the brutal colonizing sweep of the most pitiless imperial fleet, tortures us with the cynical nonchalance of a gulag functionary until even death sounds like a welcome *emergency stop* button on an efficient but pointless machine—well, what should we do? Flee, flee to the desert!

If we feel this way about the world in which we live, we are not the first. In 1 Kings 9, confronted with the murderous, blasphemous threat of Jezebel's messenger, Elijah fled for his life into the desert. In the fourth and fifth centuries Anthony and the other desert fathers, seeing society as a suicidal shipwreck,[1] quit their worldly posts and fled, seeking salvation in the desert. Arsenius, at the top of the contemporary corporate ladder, tutoring in Emperor Theodosius's household, left his comfortable position guided by a threefold injunction from a divine voice: *flee, be silent, pray.*[2]

And now the voice of a contemporary prophet whose ears rung with the suicidal overtones of his twentieth century society (which has become our own in the twenty-first) posthumously and prophetically summons us to the desert.[3] During his lifetime, his oeuvre continually repeated Jonah's warning cry, "Yet forty days!"[4] His sociological studies interrogated the present, naming *technique*—the chief element in a veritable new religion in which efficiency, productivity, control, and progress functionally replace traditional deities—as the determinative factor in an increasingly impersonal societal evolution. His theological essays addressed the individual reader, inviting them to a confrontation with the present Word of God in Holy Scripture, calling them to abandon their slavery to technical logic, to reassert their freedom in dialogue with God, and to rediscover their neighbor. Now, some forty years after he mourned the apparent inefficacy of his own prophetic warnings,[5] the appearance of his essay on "The Desert" (alongside other theological and sociological projections of lean times ahead for western institutional Christianity) strikes me as a providential provision.[6] If we have the wisdom to earnestly pray Arsenius's prayer—

1. I have borrowed these words from Thomas Merton's writings on the desert fathers. I am no expert on the fathers, but given Merton's 1960s writing date, it is worth wondering if his reading is not inflected by the societal upheavals happening around him. At times, his description of the fourth century monks sounds more akin to 1960s anti-establishment culture. See Merton, *Wisdom of the Desert*, 3.

2. This story comes from Nouwen, *Way of the Heart*, 14–15. Nouwen's small book interestingly mentions both Merton and Ellul as possible sources for wisdom before turning to the desert fathers. Of course, Nouwen could not have known of Ellul's desert essay. I follow Nouwen in structuring my own reflections around this ethical trio, though with what I hope is a somewhat less mystical accent than either Nouwen or Merton.

3. "If we let ourselves be carried along by the current of history, we will have chosen . . . the power of suicide that lies at the world's heart." Ellul, *Presence in the Modern World*, 25.

4. The full phrase from Jonah 3:4 reads: "Forty days more, and Nineveh shall be overthrown!" Ellul, *Judgement of Jonah*; Ellul, *La foi au prix du doute*; the Jonah reference in the title is lost in the English translation: Ellul, *Living Faith*.

5. Ellul casts himself as a negative image of Jonah, mourning the failure of his own communication: "I saw correctly, I spoke, I gave warning—it all went for nothing." Ellul, *Living Faith*, 212.

6. Vazquez, "Up to the Challenge," 21–27. Vazquez, Chief Enrollment Management

"Lord, lead me in the way of salvation"—this timely unearthing of old treasures invites us to reconsider Arsenius's ethical trio for our own times (which, incidentally, mirrors Elijah's own response quite closely). What might these three injunctions—flee, be silent, pray always—have to offer us?

I propose to respond to (instead of to answer) these questions with a meditation examining Elijah's desert flight in 1 Kings 19 through this ethical trio. In doing so, I will add a particularly Ellulian flavor by using my own English translation of the French translation of the Bible by André Chouraqui, a striking poetic translation whose praises Ellul sung on many occasions.[7] Each of the following three sections will thus begin with my own version of Chouraqui's text.[8]

Flee!

> Ahab informs Jezebel of everything Elijah had done
> And that he killed them, all the inspired ones with the sword.
> Jezebel sends a messenger to Elijah. He says:
> "Elohim will do likewise and more
> At this hour, tomorrow, I will have made your being
> Similar to the being of one of them."
> He sees, he gets up and goes from his being.
> He comes to Beer-sheba in Judah.
> He leaves his servant there.
> He himself goes into the desert, a day's journey.
> He comes and sits down under a broom tree

Officer at Wheaton College (IL), compiles demographic data from several articles and reports which offer predictions of challenging times ahead especially for regional (as opposed to nationally or internationally outstanding) North American institutions. In some cases, the data suggest 2025 as the "cliff" of this drop, coming eighteen years after the 2008 economic recession. Theologically, the robust and rigorous engagement in Amy J. Erickson's *Ephraim Radner, Hosean Wilderness, and the Church in the Post-Christendom West* evaluates and prophetically responds to the Western church's current institutional state drawing on the prophetic book of Hosea.

7. For more on Ellul and Chouraqui, see my introduction and Ellul's own endorsement of Chouraqui's translation in Rollison, *Jacques Ellul and the Bible*.

8. Chouraqui, *La Bible*, 117–19. Unlike Chouraqui, I have used conventional English spellings for names in my translation. By choice and method, Chouraqui's text is intentionally unfamiliar to the contemporary reader, even in French (whence, for example, the English translation of "inspired one" where "prophet" would have been a more standard rendering).

He demands death for his being and says:
"Enough!
Now, YHWH, take my being!
I am no better than my fathers."
He lays down. He sleeps under a broom tree.
And behold, a messenger touches him. He says to him:
"Get up! Eat!"
He looks and behold:
Near his head a cake cooked over coals and a jar of water.
He eats, drinks, sits and lies down.
The messenger of YHWH returns a second time.
He touches him and says:
"Get up! Eat.
Yes, long is the road for you!"
He gets up, eats and drinks.
He goes in the strength of this food
Forty days and forty nights,
To the mountain of Elohim, to Horeb. (1 Kgs 19:1–8)

If Elijah flees Israel, leaving his servant in Beersheba before quitting the promised land for the desert—effectively going back in time, reversing his people's history—he does not do so lightly. It is not a fear-driven flight; the text all but insists that fear was *not* Elijah's motivation. Indeed, the previous chapter showed just how courageous he is, having successfully challenged hundreds of prophets of Baal to a divine showdown. No, he flees because it is not humanly possible to continue. The battle is out of his hands. After the prophet of YHWH and Ahab, king of Israel, mutually accused one another for causing Israel's current turmoil, Ahab complained to Jezebel. Her response elevates the argument. She invokes *Elohim* in support of her intention to eliminate Elijah. As Hezekiah's merit was to recognize that, when political threats become blasphemously spiritual authoritarian claims, he as king was out of his depth, so Elijah's flight into the desert might be read as recognition that the fight was no longer his own.[9] In such cases, human means no longer suffice. Simple human language cannot respond anymore. Only a divine word can answer a false divinity. Only the living God's response can decide between true and false invocations of this God. And Elijah knows he won't hear God by waiting around in Israel; he is *alone*. The prophets are dead (killed by the sword); the priesthood is defunct (God's altars are destroyed); and God's covenant is abandoned. The people

9. Ellul offers this reading of Hezekiah in Ellul, *Politics of God and the Politics of Man*, 162–89.

who should belong to God have forgotten their first love, abandoned their husband, forgotten their desert marriage vows, and become whores.[10] The institutions graciously given to them to sustain their communal life with God in holiness are now twisted into political means, their purposes are perverted, and their transcendent reference inverted. Instead of mediating expiation, offering worship, and facilitating communion, the priesthood subjugated the nation to empty ephemeral idols in their nothingness. Instead of establishing the royal throne in justice, the political structures of the day turned predatory, employing even references to God in their consolidation of self-serving power.

So Elijah flees! Instead of remaining with the co-opted king and priest, the prophet flees into the desert. "Enough! Now, YHWH, take my life! I am no better than my fathers." As you took the lives of our desert-wandering ancestors who were unfit for the promised land, take my life. Exhausted, despairing, and profoundly lonely, Elijah collapses under a broom tree.[11] The promised land, the covenant—all are defiled, broken, and failed; only Elijah remains. Israel might have well have stayed in the desert.

As long as we are content to count church attendance or giving, belonging to a certain denomination, application of a given morality, adherence to an ostensibly correct doctrine, or an allegedly Christian institution, government, ruler, etc. (of any party or affiliation whatsoever), as sufficient indication in itself of God's presence, we will never flee to the desert. We will continue to seek whatever functional consolation and compromise we can with the existing order of things, however legitimate our possibilities in this role might be (like Obadiah in 1 Kings 18, hiding true prophets while outwardly continuing to serve corrupt Ahab). As long as we are content with some form of syncretic Christendom, we will never take up the challenge of reworking old forms; the inertia of tradition will be enough to triangulate a Christian ethic, even should the whole of society reorient itself in the meanwhile. If Christianity as a myth, as a cultural heritage,

10. The importance of the *covenant* as a divine betrothal of God and his people (in French, the word *alliance* covers both the English *covenant* and *marriage*) is highlighted especially in Neher, *L'essence du prophétisme*, 223–31. On p. 227, Neher writes: "The wedding or, more precisely, the first conjugal encounter, is situated in the desert, after the Exodus, before entering into Canaan."

11. As far as I can tell, the broom tree is mentioned only two other times in Scripture, in Job 30:4 and Psalm 120:4. Without twisting the texts, its use here seems to straddle both occurrences: Elijah's status as a societal outcast reflects its use in Job, while its status as an instrument of judgement in Psalms foreshadows the judgement might foreshadow Jezebel's judgement.

as a distant foundation of western freedom, as the ground for universal morality and human rights, as a worldview, as the courage of being, as a discourse, as a religion—in short, as anything less than lived dialogue with the living God—is enough, then there is no need to abuse ourselves with an ascetic desert retreat. But if we lose sleep pondering the possibility of our carrying on all the same while the living God quietly ducks out of our church services, no longer hampers our politics with prophetic critiques, withdraws from our familial, national, and transnational projects—if we can shake out of our overstimulated coma, set aside our image-curating projects, abandon the hopeless criterion of relevance, and devote ourselves to a disciplined search for the presence of God in our *hic et nunc*—then life in the uninhabitable desert suddenly seems more attractive.

But where will we find a desert today? Even if we should get lost outside of Alexandria, the old deserts are not what they used to be. Indeed, geography—space—is not what it used to be. Since Cain the lifelong nomad built his first city, there has been an irreparable mismatch between human geographical space and the space delineated by trust in God's Word. This process has only continued since the building of *Enoch*, Cain's first city, the name of which translates as: *initiation*.[12] Once the first combustion-propelled projectile levelled a city's defenses, the city abandoned its walls; we might say that through this military advance, the city *overflowed* its walls. Today with the smartphone, "We carry the city with us," in our pocket.[13] Not that the city in-itself is evil, but at least since Cain, it has been difficult for the human creature to dissociate our projects from our gods—all the more so when they are explicit rejections of divinely decreed nomadism! And when the people of YHWH are conscripted in the construction of Egyptian cities by a divine Pharaoh, the slavery involved here includes a sacred component, an element of more than just a material city. For only a divine Liberator can rescue from a divine slavery. Before the desert can become a meaningful *geographic* space, we must first "fashion our own desert": the false divine claims of Egypt (or as in Elijah's case, Israelite civilization herself) must be desacralized.[14]

12. Ellul, *Meaning of the City*, 5.

13. Virilio, *The Administration of Fear*, 65–66: "In 20th century societies, the city was still at home, radio for example. With the new technologies, we carry the city with us." Concerning the outmoding of city walls, see Virilio, *Speed and Politics*, 11.

14. Nouwen, *Way of the Heart*, 31.

Easier said than done! Deeper even than physical labor is the slavery which roots in our own hearts, the bondage which causes us to yearn for Egypt even as we leave it. As for us, if our constructed digital and economic world remains a humble human riff on God's own space-time—wonderful! But if Ellul is right, then against the unprecedented power offered to the average individual by the affordable appendage of the smartphone, the Apple watch, etc., then avoiding such slavery means we must discipline ourselves more rigorously than all our ancestors. If in the electronic age Ellul could already write humans had "lost their souls in the perfect whir of their engine," then in our day the work of desacralization will truly require "an asceticism without precedent."[15] For the microprocessor outpaced the engine when it made it possible to travel immense distances without having to actually move geographically. Now, space comes to us.

Solitude, then, is the battleground where the fight for desacralization is fought. Certainly, nothing has changed since Pascal. We still don't know how to go sit in a room alone for an hour.[16] If anything, it has gotten worse because Pascal's room didn't even have Wi-Fi. But if "our desert today is the crowd,"[17] withdrawal into solitude is a precondition for changing this desert from societal wasteland to a place of encounter. As Christ often purposely broke up the crowds who came to him or simply slipped away in search of prayer in solitude, so we, as heirs to the era of the mass production of everything—including ideas and opinions—need be alone for a while, to

15. See Ellul, *Presence in the Modern World*, 59. The second citation comes from Ellul, "Faut-il se conformer au siècle present?," 4–5: "But what should we do, then? More precisely, we should ask ourselves the question: *what should we be?* We must be ready to live through a period of spiritual solitude. Our desert today is the crowd. Our Christianity will thus involve a rigor, an asceticism without precedent" (my translation).

16. "All the unhappiness of men arises from one single fact, that they cannot stay quietly in their own chamber." Pascal, *Pensées*, 39 (§139). Cf. Nouwen, *Making All Things New*, 70: "As soon as we are alone . . . inner chaos opens up in us. This chaos can be so disturbing and so confusing that we can hardly wait to get busy again. Entering a private room and shutting the door, therefore, does not mean that we immediately shut out all our inner doubts, anxieties, fears, bad memories, unresolved conflicts, angry feelings and impulsive desires. On the contrary, when we have removed our outer distraction, we often find that our inner distractions manifest themselves to us in full force. We often use the outer distractions to shield ourselves from the interior noises. This makes the discipline of solitude all the more important." See also Kierkegaard's fruitful suggestion that Christianity is simply obedient living rooted in talking with God, reading the Bible, and praying while locked alone in our room alone: Zachmann, "Kierkegaard on Language," 29–48.

17. Cf. n. 15 above.

feel the void we've been avoiding by immersing ourselves in work, distraction, business, activity, or even community. The bad news is that the noise of the city is closer and more deafening than ever. The good news is that shutting it out might be as simple as turning off your phone and unplugging your router for a while. We do not perfectly coincide with our place in social networks, neither digital nor 'real'; flight into solitude can throw this poor fit into sharper relief. Only by recovering true solitude can we hope to remember who we are *outside* of our virtual togetherness, especially when, as for Elijah, this togetherness is so often a lie.

Even here, fortunately, the work does not begin with us. Happily, solitude is not forever. Solitude is not magic. It is not a meditative technique for finding God. It is a very human first step in a desperate search, a step into the void, an opening to which God responds. It is a necessary moment for encounter to be possible, a separation which alone can look for a way to make togetherness meaningful again.[18]

The text emphasizes the blasphemy of Jezebel's threat by paralleling it to God's own approach to Elijah. As Jezebel sends a messenger to divinely threaten Elijah's life, YHWH sends a messenger to encourage Elijah, to call him even deeper into the desert than he thought he would need to go, to prepare him to go further than he could go on his own. This angelic messenger *touches* Elijah, graciously offering him bread and water, and raises him up. Elijah eats and drinks; sits, then lays down again, lacking the strength to stay awake. Again the messenger—this time specified as YHWH's own messenger—awakens him; *get up*, *eat* and *drink—long is your journey*. Without this gracious message, how could Elijah know how far he had to wander, what would be required of him, much less actually have the strength to do it? From the very beginning, let there be no illusions: the desert is only livable by the freely given grace of God.

Be Silent!

> He comes there, towards the cave: he sleeps there.
> And behold the word of YHWH [comes] to him. He says:
> "What are you doing here, Elijah?"
> He says:

18. "Somewhere we know that without silence words lose their meaning, that without listening speaking no longer heals, that without distance closeness cannot cure." Nouwen, *Out of Solitude*, 18.

"I am jealous, jealous for YHWH, Elohim Tzevaot.
Yes, they have abandoned your pact, the Children of Israel.
They have destroyed your altars,
They have killed your inspired ones with the sword.
I have remained, I alone.
And they seek my being, to take it."
He says:
"Go out. Stand on the mountain, before YHWH."
And behold: YHWH passes by.
A wind, big and strong, dismantles the mountains,
Breaks the rocks,
Before YHWH.
No, not in the wind, YHWH.
And after the wind, an earthquake.
No, not in the earthquake, YHWH.
And after the earthquake, a fire.
No, not in the fire, YHWH.
And after the fire, a voice:
A subtle silence.
And that is when Elijah hears:
He covers his face in his robe.
He goes out and stands at the opening of the cave.
And behold a voice [comes] to him:
"What are you doing here, Elijah?"
He says:
"I am jealous, jealous for YHWH, Elohim Tzevaot.
Yes, they have abandoned your pact, the Children of Israel.
They have destroyed your altars,
They have killed your inspired ones, with the sword.
I have remained, I alone.
And they seek my being, to take it." (1 Kgs 19:9–14)

So Elijah flees by grace to the mountain of Horeb, or Sinai—that is, all the way back to Israel's origin as a people, to where she met God and the covenant was inaugurated, the political laws codified, and the pattern for the priesthood revealed. And he hides himself in a cave. Biblically, caves are often hiding places, refuges, tombs, or (for Saul) toilets—or several of these at once! Elijah retreats, having asked YHWH to take his life, into a cave in Mt. Sinai where God revealed himself, after a forty day and forty night grace-fueled journey. Desperate, exhausted, living in a tomb and only by grace, Elijah is alone.

And "Behold, a voice [came] to him: 'Elijah, what are you doing here?'"

Is this question "what did you come out to seek?" Or "what do *you* think this is?" "What are you hoping for, coming all the way out here and sleeping in a tomb?" Or "what's wrong?" Or all, or none of the above? With this voice, already Elijah is no longer alone. His cries have been heard. He now discovers that his despairing cry for death was met with an invitation. His flight from people was converted into a journey to the presence of God. This is where Elijah's flight brought him. The great gain of forty hot days and hungry nights boils down to this: a loving, personal question in a quiet voice, a touching moment of intimate divine care. Hearing this voice, this costly conversation sought like buried treasure in an empty field, was worth the journey.

"What are you doing here?" In Elijah's response we see both the driving desire which burned within him, guiding his zealous proclamation and relentless opposition to the corrupted regime, and his utter despair, his solitude—his loneliness, even. We see that he is not just solitary like a monk. He is alone like a refugee, alone like a fugitive. In fact, Elijah is the protected wanderer that Cain should have been.[19] "I am jealous, *jealous* for the Lord." However, this "I alone am left" is not derisive judgement cast down from a moral high ground. No, we have seen that Elijah is no better than his fathers. This is not "I'm morally pure, so who cares about the rest?" No—if Israel is lost, Elijah too is lost!

If we are to flee—to desacralize our enslaving idols, bringing them back to a simple block of wood, or a simple communicative network, or a simple legal framework—we find that in fleeing from false community, our retreat into solitude becomes by grace an advance towards a divine meeting. But this meeting will only be what it is if we are desperately jealous and if nothing else can slake our gnawing hunger.

Everything else must die. Every other support must go. Every other thing which makes us who we are, must be stripped away. Grace, and only grace, can sustain our strenuous ascetic flight, our rejection of all other nourishment, if we choose to fly into the desert, to positively answer an invitation to ordained discussion. No moral difference between the church and the world is decisive here; the relation between the two cuts across different lines. To be invited to this meeting, the church must love the presence of God so much that she cannot bear His crushing absence from the

19. Ellul, *Meaning of the City*, 3. Ellul points out that part of Cain's consequence of murdering his brother is becoming a restless wanderer. Cain tries to avoid this, however, because he settles down and builds a city in Nod, *the land of wandering*. Ellul spots and draws out the tragic irony here.

rest of society. If her love of God drives her to be different from society, this difference only heightens her love for the world, only amplifies her care for the fate of all others and everything. If the collapse of institutions like the priesthood or the kingdom—or the hollowed-out humanities departments of our universities, the deserted cafes and bars in the apocalyptic post COVID-19 landscape, the mechanized press whose words and opinions are bought by billionaires,[20] or the mockery of democracy that in our hearts we know our elections and trials have become—if their collapse is tragic for the Christian, it is so only because the Christian should be positively tortured by the fate of those who inhabit these institutions, scandalized at their enslavement to power and domination implicit in any idolatry. Nor let us think that this intolerance that others should be slaves should translate directly to political activism, for as with Israel, political slavery is only an outward form. Like Paul, we can sing freely even in chains. Not by her own means, by her own political engagement, will the church effect this freedom. All she can do is gamble everything, even her entire life, by fleeing into solitude, on the hope that God will meet her for a talk. Or, to paraphrase Jesus in Matthew's Gospel, those who will gamble away their life for him will win their life with him—and those who do not, will not.

In Elijah's mouth, who is no better than his fathers, these words ring like mourning, or even repentance, for he too is part of what his society has become. And so should it ring in our own mouths. If we are not ourselves deeply sorry before the face of God—sorry for every one of God's creatures lovelessly converted into a "meat product" in a lifeless assembly line,[21] sorry for every inch of spoiled earth which our unparalleled powers have transformed into a landfill,[22] sorry for how we have exported our slavery and crushing debt to far-flung continents and closed ourselves up in our wealth and luxury,[23] sorry for all but abolishing the birth of babies who don't meet imposed criteria for 'worthy' life,[24] sorry for every refugee sleeping by the

20. On the swaying effects of the Bill & Melinda Gates Foundation's investments in journalism, see Schwab, "Journalism's Gates Keepers."

21. Cf. Cavanaugh, *Being Consumed*, 29–31; cf. Brock, "On the Present Reality of Our Posthuman Future," 11.

22. During my youth, two actual mountain-sized landfills were constructed a short drive from my home. They not only mar the landscape; when the humid heat of summer comes along, their stench spreads for miles along the highway.

23. Cf. Ahn, *Just Debt*, 25–27.

24. Cf. Brock, *Wondrously Wounded*, esp. ch. 3.

roadside while police ensure they stay out of our cities;[25] if we can't see our reflection in every news report of a school shooting—if we cannot love what we see, how could we delude ourselves into thinking we love One we do not see?

And then, desperate, jealous, dead except in and by grace, Elijah receives the command: "Go out, stand on the mountain before YHWH." What happens next reveals the meaning of the command. The last words matter most: *before YHWH*. Go out before YHWH—and nothing else! Respond to no other call! Elijah now has a divine command, a spoken word calling him to by physically present before God. If God's soft voice already assuaged his loneliness, we can only imagine what standing in YHWH's very presence might add! At this point we are, very precisely, tempted to conjure all our images of God, to bring out all the metaphysical and experiential baggage which centuries of discourse and our own experiences have piled onto that term for better or for worse. In the West, we might imagine a giant, white-bearded old man striding up to the mountain. We might prefer to imagine God as a woman, an animal, an energy force, a blinding light. . . . Blend into these images our own sense of internalized guilt for having transgressed a stringent moral law, or the pain of a father-figure's abuse or abandonment, or the resentment of power-tripping former pastors and priests, or convoluted cultural memories of a brutal future judgment, all of which somehow climb the ladder of authority and are subsumed into the thought of God himself; in short, we have no idea what to expect from this meeting, but whatever it will be, it will probably involve the appearance of something fearful.

*

"And behold: YHWH passes by."

*

A wind so powerful it splits rocks (*démonte les montagnes*, in Chouraqui's French); an earthquake which shakes the foundations of everything solid and stable; a burning, consuming fire; are not these all signs of YHWH's presence? Does not the spirit blow where he wills? (John 3:8). When he

25. While I was writing this in September 2020, several French newspapers published regular updates on the overcrowded, fire and COVID-plagued refugee camps on the Greek isle of Lesbos, notably mentioning police efforts to keep refugees outside of cities. Cf. "Sur l'île grecque de Lesbos."

looks, do not the mountains quake? (Ps 104:32). Is not our God a consuming fire? (Heb 12:29). Wouldn't it have been utterly reasonable for Elijah to go out before any of these three? Would he not be justified to think that because these manifestations which Scripture itself associates with God's presence were there, God must also therefore be present?

Elijah's task is to listen. God has spoken; Elijah has replied; there has been an initial dialogue. But here, called to discern God's own presence, only silence is suitable. Only silence can make room for the necessary discernment involved in teasing the divine presence out of the promenade of frightening natural, unnatural, and even supernatural events which parade before Elijah's cave and which make up our own history. Only by attuning himself to the softly spoken divine command can Elijah be prepared to discern the divine absence at the heart of loud and powerful displays calling for his attention.

Is this not indeed the heart of our own task today? How do we even know if God is present, if He is speaking? Is it church attendance, political sway, the number of endowed chairs of theology, or overflowing literary production, a highly rated research profile, abundant ecstatic prophecies (or even miraculous healings), the right prayer spoken over wafers and wine—are any of these sufficient criteria to move us? Should our politicians all convert and "Judeo-Christian values" become the law of the land, should we then quit our cave?

At the core of these questions is a different question: "Who do you say that I am?" Is our most intimate knowledge of God ultimately closer to an earth-shattering exercise of overwhelming power? Does he reveal himself primarily in the eternal consuming fire of retributive or punitive judgement? Is the critical force to overturn ideas, societies, or civilizations the defining divine mark?

No. In Nouwen's words, "Our task is the opposite of distraction."[26] Like flight into solitude, silence is not an ascetic technique with its end in itself. It is only meaningful as a moment in dialogue, a search for and response to the presence of someone else. It is an important counterpoint to speaking which gives words some of their meaning—"the home of the Word."[27] What is not said, silences held for shorter or longer, also say something. It is a human honing of the ear, an attuning of one's capacity for discernment. Silence allows words a right relation to a presence which words

26. Nouwen, *Way of the Heart*, 63.

27. Nouwen, *Way of the Heart*, 48.

without silence often serve only to dissimulate. "In order for the word to become truly demonstrative, a kind of asceticism and interior discipline are required."[28] At issue is this: what force is strong enough to move us? Alternatively, are we disciplined enough to remain still in the face of the most crushing demonstration of power and efficiency? In today's world, can we discern the absence behind the brain research funded by advertising agencies, the void of the most riveting political propaganda, and the emptiness in our art? Can we resist all the false images of God and ourselves, to respond only to the voice whose very speech is a "subtle silence," the "silence of a vanishing murmur"?[29] Can we hear the whisper of God when God is whispering, calling us into the desert?

In the story of Elijah, the cataclysmic events documented in the text do not reveal God to Elijah. God's whisper reveals God to Elijah. All the images we conjure fail and fall. God's quiet speech is God's loving presence. If this voice is absent, all the wind, fire, and earthquakes in the world offer us nothing. Elijah the prophet is not hunted by fear or enslaved by power. In the end, the heart of what he is reveals itself to be a simple, quiet dialogue with God. If asceticism is a question today, it is because hearing is harder than ever. Silence names the disciplined freedom of patient listening that responds only to the still small voice of God's love.

The glorious irony of this text is that Elijah had everything from the beginning. God's passing by does nothing to alter God's presence as present in God's Word. The dialogue after the three trials mirrors the dialogue which preceded them. Nothing has changed in the mode of God's presence or the attention He gives to Elijah's affairs. Nothing has changed in what Elijah has to say to God. And this is precisely the point. Let the powers that be rage and act out, let them serve the power they seek; God is not moved nor co-opted by their discourse. God, I am that I am (Exod 3:14), is the same, yesterday, today, and forever (Heb 13:8). God's quiet presence with Elijah is both the precondition for and the outcome of all of his seeking. There is nothing to add, nothing to accomplish; "all flesh is grass . . . but the word of our God will stand forever" (Isa 40:6–8). And whether it speaks in the blood of the persecuted global church or in the deafening silence

28. Ellul, *Humiliation of the Word*, 133.

29. Ellul borrows this last phrase from a French translation of 1 Kings 19:12 and uses it in his short, personal article explaining who Jesus Christ is for him. The article finishes thus: "The one who has the (only) words of eternal life meets me in my uncertainty. And it all happens 'in the silence of a vanishing murmur' (1 Kings 19:12)." Ellul, "Jésus Christ," 19–20.

audible in cacophonous western culture, this same voice is our guide and goal, the only conversation which makes anything else worthwhile. "Because your love is better than life" (Ps 63:3).

Pray Always!

> "Go. Return on your way, to the Desert to Damascus.
> And come: anoint Hazael, as king over Aram.
> Jehu son of Nimshi, anoint him as king over Israel.
> Elisha son of Shaphat, of Abel-meholah,
> Anoint him as an inspired one, in your place." (1 Kgs 19:15–16)

Flight, silence, the ascetic work of disciplined listening—all this is precursor to and part of prayer. Prayer is not saying words about God to God. Prayer is a life lived before God, a life which audaciously expects God to pay attention, to want to live with us, too. Prayer names this ridiculous dialogue which sets any poor fool higher than any ruler, any slave higher than every master, because in prayer my life claims to matter dearly to the God who is higher than any height, precisely because he descended lower than any depth. "Where can I flee from your presence?" (Ps 139:7). Prayer spans the space-time rift between the wandering nomad and the stationary city she inhabits, between God's decreed intention and my present reality. As the external observer might think that Elijah simply holed up in a cave to sleep off his fatigued fear before returning to his work refreshed, prayer changes everything while leaving everything the same. As Onesimus can run away in flight and return home, the same slave to the same master, Paul's intervening invocation of the relation of Jesus Christ to both master and slave means that neither can be what they once were.

Indeed, this is the element of risk, the danger of prayer. Do we really think that an encounter with the living God can leave us unchanged? Can we dream of a desperate desert flight in search of God's presence that would send us back home unscathed? Jacob's violent search for divine blessing was a success that left him limping; Elijah, too, finds what he is looking for, fulfilling every exacting jot and tittle of his request. "Take my life . . ." and so God does. God hears his cry, notes his ardent desire for divine presence, even to the point of death. In their desert dialogue, God calls Elijah out of the tomb where he had hidden himself for one last mission: to anoint replacements, both for Jezebel and for himself. Elijah gets what he was seeking. He finishes caught up in an ascending wind, separated from Elisha by fire. But he pays for it with his ministry, his job, indeed, his earthly existence altogether. Elijah has no need to pass through death; he already has. When Ellul writes that the entire Christian life takes place in the desert, we can thus hear the echo of "take up your cross . . ." Like Solzhenitsyn in the gulag, the only way to survive this voyage is to be dead already.[30]

Today, as in Ellul's day, prayer tends to fall by the wayside.[31] Many believe we should pray; few do.[32] The call to prayer, for Nouwen, is an invitation to divine rest; in prayer, the sought object is found in an already which does not exhaust the not yet. The presence made present in the promise fuels the hope looking for its fulness in the future. The invitation to pray is a call to join in the work of the priesthood of all believers, continually burning a pleasing incense in God's holy presence. It is the call to live the prophetic freedom of the Word, testifying to the utter sufficiency of God's grace for all of life. And it is simultaneously the call to leave the ever-growing incessant projects in which "the rich will fade away" (Jas 1:11), to exit the frenetic business of our personal and professional development, to become instead welcome guests at a prepared royal feast. Prayer transforms impersonal and accelerated atomic time to the rhythm of divine dialogue; it changes the global digital grid, converting astronomical expanses into speaking distance with God. And it all happens "in the whisper of a murmur."

30. Cf. Solzhenitsyn, *Gulag Archipelago*, 130: "What do you need to make you stronger than the interrogator and the whole trap? From the moment you go to prison you must put your cozy past firmly behind you. At the very threshold, you must say to yourself: 'My life is over, a little early to be sure, but there's nothing to be done about it. I shall never return to freedom. I am condemned to die—now or a little later. But later on, in truth, it will be even harder, and so the sooner the better. I no longer have any property whatsoever. For me those I love have died, and for them I have died.'"

31. Ellul's reason for writing *Prayer and Modern Man*—more aptly titled *Impossible Prayer* in the original French—is precisely that humanity neither prays nor seeks to pray. As often elsewhere, Ellul writes first of and to himself. Ellul, *Prayer and Modern Man*.

32. Nouwen, *Way of the Heart*, 71.

Conclusion

Peregrinato est tacere; silence makes us pilgrims.[33] Today more than ever, since we are already immersed in the space-time "desert of the real,"[34] one need hardly leave home to find the desert in one way or another. If it feels like society is falling apart around you, do not let it remain a simple wasteland. Flee to the desert, and you may find that in fact you were invited there in the first place. Be silent—that is, listen for where and when the divine voice is (and—which is more difficult—is not) leading you. You were brought into the desert so that God could speak sweetly to you. This encounter is not for anyone; or rather, it is. The call goes out, but only those with no life anywhere else can truly respond to it.

33. Nouwen, *Way of the Heart*, 50. The character of silence/pilgrimage contrasts notably with the pair blabbering/wandering aimlessly: "a blabbermouth wanders aimless over the earth." Benedict, *Rule*, 53. Venarde marks the Latin citation as coming from Psalm 139/140:12.

34. The iconic phrase "Welcome to the Desert of the Real" spoken by Morpheus in the 1999 blockbuster film *The Matrix* inaugurated the twentieth century on multiple levels. First, the phrase heralded the new century some twenty years in advance: it refers to the opening pages of Jean Baudrillard's 1981 book *Simulacres et simulation*, which in turn offers a spin on a fable by Jorge Luis Borges. In Borges' fable, cartographers make a life-size map that literally overlays the empire which it renders; the map later falls into ruin, and its remaining fragments can be found in the desert. Baudrillard writes that for us, the territory-map relation is inverted: the map today is more fundamental than the territory, and the remains of "*the desert of the real itself*" can be found in the simulated map-world in which we live. Next, the stunning visual rendering of this metaphor in *The Matrix* popularized philosophical and technological questions of the construction of real-life experiences, durably installing the phrase into our cultural vocabulary. Finally, philosopher Slavoj Žižek used the phrase shortly afterward as the title of an essay collection responding to the terrorist attacks on the World Trade Center in New York on September 11, 2001. Baudrillard had already made a strong connection between this simulated map-world and American culture, treating the elaborately constructed happy dream-world of Disneyland as a microcosm for the entire USA; now Žižek saw in the collapse of the two towers an event with dream-shattering capacity (akin to Neo's rude awakening by Morpheus), a glitch in the isolated "American sphere of safety"—in short, a revelatory moment *par excellence* for the West as a whole. In this latter sense, the COVID-19 pandemic really does serve as revelation of something true about the fears and tendencies of a given people. For example, March 2020 (the first major media peak of the COVID-19 pandemic), the US experienced "the second busiest month ever for gun sales"—a unique response which seems to reflect fears of civil unrest. Cf. Baudrillard, *Simulacres et simulation*, 10; Žižek, *Welcome to the Desert of the Real*; Collins and Yaffe-Bellany, "About 2 Million Guns Were Sold."

If God is indeed silent or absent,[35] it is not because we no longer know how or where to look for him, but rather because our slavery is quite comfortable. We are happy enough with cities full of imitation gods, so why bother venturing into the desert to find him? But if we can become jealous, jealous for God as God is jealous for us, such that we are no longer sated by mere theology, nor by whatever semblance of communion our broken institutions can provide us, then there is hope. For in tension with Jonah's "Yet forty days," with the prophetic warning of Jeremiah—"Take warning, O Jerusalem, or I shall turn from you in disgust, and make you a desolation, an uninhabited land" (6:8)—Jeremiah's own prophetic promise still holds true (along with the song it sings to our hard-of-hearing ears): "When you search for me, you will find me; if you seek me with all your heart" (Jer 29:13).

Bibliography

Ahn, Ilsup. *Just Debt: Theology, Ethics, and Neoliberalism.* Waco, TX: Baylor University Press, 2017.

Baudrillard, Jean. *Simulacres et simulation.* Paris: Editions Galilée, 1981.

Benedict. *The Rule of Saint Benedict.* Edited and translated by Bruce L. Venarde. Dumbarton Oaks Medieval Library 6. Cambridge, MA: Harvard University Press, 2011.

Brock, Brian. "On the Present Reality of Our Posthuman Future." In *Being Human in a Technological Age: Rethinking Theological Anthropology*, edited by Van den Heuvel, 3–22. Leuven: Peeters, 2020.

———. *Wondrously Wounded: Theology, Disability, and the Body of Christ.* Studies in Religion, Theology, and Disability. Waco, TX: Baylor University Press, 2019.

Cavanaugh, William. *Being Consumed: Economics and Christian Desire.* Grand Rapids: Eerdmans, 2008.

Chouraqui, André. *La Bible: Traduite et présentée par André Chouraqui: Rois 1.* Paris: Desclée de Brouwer, 1975.

Collins, Keith, and David Yaffe-Bellany. "About 2 Million Guns Were Sold in the U.S. as Virus Fears Spread." *The New York Times*, April 1, 2020. https://www.nytimes.com/interactive/2020/04/01/business/coronavirus-gun-sales.html.

Ellul, Jacques. "Faut-il se conformer au siècle present?" *Paix et liberté* 68 (1968) 4–5.

———. *Hope in Time of Abandonment.* Translated by C. Edward Hopkin. Eugene, OR: Wipf & Stock, 2012.

———. *The Humiliation of the Word.* Translated by Joyce Main Hanks. Grand Rapids: Eerdmans, 1985.

———."Jésus Christ." *Table Ronde* 250 (1968) 19–20.

35. Ellul argued that we are living through a period of God's silence in Ellul, *Hope in Time of Abandonment.*

———. *The Judgement of Jonah*. Translated by Geoffrey W. Bromiley. Eugene, OR: Wipf & Stock, 2011.

———. *La foi au prix du doute: Encore quarante jours . . .* Paris: La Table Ronde, 2015.

———. *Living Faith: Belief and Doubt in a Perilous World*. Translated by Peter Heinegg. San Francisco: Harper & Row, 1983.

———. *The Meaning of the City*. Translated by Dennis Pardee. Grand Rapids: Eerdmans, 1970.

———. *The Politics of God and the Politics of Man*. Translated by Geoffrey W. Bromiley. Grand Rapids: Eerdmans, 1972.

———. *Prayer and Modern Man*. Translated by C. Edward Hopkin. New York: Seabury, 1970.

———. *Presence in the Modern World*. Translated by Lisa Richmond. Eugene, OR: Cascade, 2016.

Erickson, Amy J. *Ephraim Radner, Hosean Wilderness, and the Church in the Post-Christendom West*. Brill Studies in Systematic Theology 22. Leiden: Brill, 2020.

Merton, Thomas. *The Wisdom of the Desert: Sayings from the Desert Fathers of the Fourth Century*. New York: New Directions, 1960.

Neher, André. *L'essence du prophétisme*. Paris: Calmann-Lévy, 1972.

Nouwen, Henri. *Making All Things New: An Invitation to the Spiritual Life*. San Francisco: Harper & Row, 1981.

———. *Out of Solitude: Three Meditations on the Christian Life*. Notre Dame: Ave Maria, 2008.

———. *The Way of the Heart: Desert Spirituality and Contemporary Ministry*. San Francisco: Harper & Row, 1981.

Pascal, Blaise. *Pensées of Blaise Pascal*. Translated by W. F. Trotter. Everyman's Library 874. London: Dent & Sons, 1947.

Rollison, Jacob Marques, ed. *Jacques Ellul and the Bible: Towards a Hermeneutic of Freedom*. Eugene, OR: Pickwick, 2020.

Schwab, Tim. "Journalism's Gates Keepers." *Columbia Journalism Review*, August 21, 2020. https://www.cjr.org/criticism/gates-foundation-journalism-funding.php.

Solzhenitsyn, Aleksandr. *The Gulag Archipelago, 1918–1956: An Experiment in Literary Investigation*. Vols. 1–2. New York: Harper & Row, 1974.

"Sur l'île grecque de Lesbos, la majorité des migrants installés dans un nouveau camp." *Le Monde*, September 19, 2020. https://www.lemonde.fr/international/article/2020/09/19/sur-l-ile-grecque-de-lesbos-la-majorite-des-migrants-installes-dans-un-nouveau-camp_6052862_3210.html.

Vazquez, Silvio E. "Up to the Challenge: Addressing the Shifting Landscape of Christian Higher Education." *Wheaton Magazine* 22 (2019) 21–27.

Virilio, Paul. *The Administration of Fear*. Translated by Ames Hodges. Intervention series 10. Los Angeles: Semiotext(e), 2012.

———. *Speed and Politics: An Essay on Dromology*. Translated by Mark Polizzotti. Foreign Agents Series. San Francisco: Semiotext(e), 1986.

The Wachowski Brothers, dir. *The Matrix*. Burbank, CA: Warner Bros. Pictures, 1999.

Zachmann, Randall C. "Kierkegaard on Language: Peril and Promise." In *T&T Clark Companion to the Theology of Kierkegaard*, edited by Aaron P. Edwards and David J. Gouwens, 29–48. London: T&T Clark, 2020.

Žižek, Slavoj. *Welcome to the Desert of the Real*. London: Verso, 2013.

Printed and bound by CPI Group (UK) Ltd, Croydon, CR0 4YY

11/08/2026

14939925-0013